UNDERSTANDING

THE YOUNG HORSE

YOUR **GUIDE** TO HORSE HEALTH
CARE AND MANAGEMENT

ISBN 1-58150-038-6

Printed in the United States of America

First Edition: November 1999

1 2 3 4 5 6 7 8 9 10

UNDERSTANDING

THE YOUNG HORSE

YOUR **GUIDE** TO HORSE HEALTH
CARE AND MANAGEMENT

By Les Sellnow

The Blood-Horse, Inc. Lexington, KY

Contents

INTRODUCTION

A great many books have been written on training horses. Thousands of magazine articles have been printed on the same subject. Every spring a multitude of clinics address one phase of training or another.

Much of the information presented and techniques demonstrated at clinics, along with many of the books and articles, are excellent. Very often the writers and clinicians are knowledgeable horsemen and women who have been very successful in the approaches they espouse.

This book is not designed to present startling new information about how to start a young horse in training. Actually, there really is nothing new — it's all a matter of applying what has been known by good horsemen for centuries. That is what is offered here — a discussion of how to apply the available knowledge.

There has been a trend in recent years by a number of clinicians to demonstrate how you can start the training process in the morning with a young horse that has never been saddled and be riding it before the day is out. Many of these clinicians are very successful in their approach and the finely tuned horses they turn out attest to their ability. The inherent danger to the nonprofessional horseman is that he or she might feel confident in letting a young horse go untouched for the first two years or more of its life, then decide to train it in one or two days. This approach for anyone but an experienced trainer is a wreck waiting to happen.

While I do not take issue with any of the techniques offered by most reputable trainers and clinicians, I do believe there is another way to approach training a horse that is particularly suited to the nonprofessional. I refer to it as the building block method. Each training step, beginning right after birth, is a building block. Only when a block of knowledge or response is firmly established do we add another block or level. If we use this approach, beginning at infancy, and on through the horse's formative years, we will have an equine companion who will be responsive, enjoy the tasks it performs, and seek to please its handler.

This, I believe, is the ideal approach. However, we must remember that horses are individuals and must be treated as such during the training process. We must be ready to be flexible in our methods. The building blocks will vary. When training, we must learn to recognize and properly interpret the subtle signals that the young horse gives us, then react in an appropriate manner.

There is no room for abuse in this approach. None. However, the trainer must always be the dominant figure in the horse's life because that is the way the horse's social structure is patterned. Only when we achieve the role of "dominant horse" will we have the full attention, trust, and respect of the animal being trained.

Timing is key to success. We must know when to admonish or discipline and when to praise.

By using the building block method, anyone who truly enjoys horses and understands how and why they react as they do can be successful in training the young equine.

Les Sellnow
Riverton, Wyoming

CHAPTER 1

Building Block Training

Horse training is a thinking person's game. That may sound a bit simplistic, or even arrogant, but it is true. Training a horse at any level of development or age requires total concentration on the trainer's part. Unless a trainer is cognizant of every subtle signal in the horse's communicative repertoire, he or she might miss something that could be instrumental in the animal's ability to learn and respond during the training process.

Horse training requires patience and quiet, even-handed treatment of the student. There is no room for anger. None. When we become angry, we make mistakes that could have a lifelong effect on the horse's psyche. It is easy to anthropomorphize — to attribute human personality to something nonhuman, such as the horse. When we do this, anger easily can be the result because when things go wrong, we might believe that the "horse should know better" or "is deliberately making life miserable" for us. Instead, the animal simply might be reacting to incorrect stimuli on our part.

Horse training requires consistency. The horse does not have the gift of cognitive thinking. If we pet it one day for doing something, but give it a slap for doing the same thing later on, the horse only knows that the same behavior elicited two totally different responses and will be confused.

An example would be the young foal we find to be so cute when it nibbles on a coat sleeve or tugs at a coattail with its teeth. Later, when those same teeth include a pinch of skin with the jacket sleeve, the knee-jerk reaction might be to whack the youngster alongside the head with the flat of our hand.

Thus, training also involves teaching the horse at an early age what it must not do as well as what it should do. If you don't want the adult horse to be a biter, do not allow the youngster ever to learn that biting is an option.

> ## AT A GLANCE
>
> • Horse training requires patience; there is no room for anger.
>
> • The building block method is an excellent tool for the nonprofessional horse handler.
>
> • Building block training should begin early in a foal's life.
>
> • During the first week to 10 days of a foal's life, repeat the handling process on a daily basis.

I refer to all of the lessons learned by a horse during training — both what it should do and what it should not do — as building blocks. Each block that becomes firmly established provides a base of support for the next block.

The building block method can be an excellent tool for a person who is not an expert at handling horses. If trouble develops with a certain "block," the training procedure can be halted until that specific problem is solved. Sometimes this might involve help from a professional.

START THE PROCESS EARLY

Building block training should begin early in the foal's life. Dr. Robert Miller of California has authored a book, *Imprint Training of the Newborn Foal*, and prepared a video on imprint training. Imprint training is perhaps the best single way to get a young foal started in the training process early in life.

The only shortcoming is that there is a narrow window of opportunity to apply the imprint training method. It must be done in the very first hours of the youngster's life to be completely effective. In many cases that might not be possible. For example, you might go out to the barn in the morning and find that the foal was born hours earlier and is already on its feet and nursing.

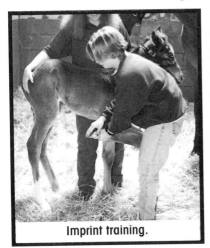

Imprint training.

Then, too, the majority of horse owners are not full-time breeders. Raising horses often is more hobby than business. This means that they might have time that first morning to dip the navel in iodine, make certain the mare has passed the afterbirth, put down fresh bedding, and determine that the foal has no visible signs of illness — then have to leave for work.

This means that the foal will not be touched again by human hands until that evening. Although a bond still can be established with the youngster, it may not be quite as effective as imprinting during those first hours after birth.

By the time the foal is a day or more old, it will already have learned to be somewhat wary of intruders. If its dam is protective, seeking to place her body between the handler and her foal, the youngster will be receiving a signal that the human might pose a threat to its well-being.

The best approach to the first "training" session with the new foal does depend somewhat on the dam's attitude. It is desirable that the mare show strong maternal instincts, but not to the degree that she attacks whomever or whatever enters the stall. If the mare is overly aggressive, she should be tied off to the side while you work with the foal.

When dealing with a first-time equine mother, use caution when first entering the stall. Even the most docile of mares has been known to become over-protective and attack with snapping teeth, even when someone well-known to her first steps into the stall.

The best case scenario is a mare that welcomes the

handler's approach and allows him or her to work with the foal and not interfere.

A good way to begin a training session is to cradle the foal gently in your arms — one arm across the chest, the other at the buttocks. The goal is to get the foal to stand still. By using an arm at the chest and another across the rear, you are forming a barrier against either forward or backward progress. The foal likely will struggle when finding itself imprisoned. The goal should be to control the foal gently within the cradle of your arms, not wrestle it to the ground. The moment you can free the arm at the foal's buttocks, your fingers should immediately begin gently scratching its withers and croup.

This technique or approach is learned from the horses themselves. Where do horses often scratch each other with their teeth when buddied up on a pleasant day? On the withers and over the point of the croup. These are spots where gentle massage elicits a feeling of pleasure and contentment in the horse. By scratching the young foal at the withers and the croup, we are imitating equine behavior.

Soon, the foal will be enjoying the treatment and will stand in one place, wanting even more. Once the youngster is relaxed and standing quietly, we continue our ministrations. Now is the time to rub your hands along the neck, over the poll and down the foal's face. The poll is extremely sensitive with a lot of nerve endings just beneath the skin. The foal should be desensitized to being touched at the poll very early in its life. Failure to firmly establish this "building block" could result in a horse that is difficult to bridle. In the early stages, don't put any pressure on the poll. Instead, caress it gently with the fingertips. Once the foal accepts having its poll touched and massaged, add another dimension. Now is the time for gentle persuasion. Use your fingers to apply a gentle squeezing pressure on the poll. This will cause the youngster to lower its head. The moment it does so, relax the pressure and caress the area again with the palm of the hand.

Later in life, when it is time for bridling, you will only have to lay an arm — the one holding the bridle — between the horse's ears and it will lower its head for the bit. This reaction is far better than the "giraffe" move when the horse raises its mouth up and out of reach.

Your hands also should travel gently over the face and muzzle, beneath the jaw and along the underside of the neck. At this stage of its life, the foal, when completely relaxed, might want to suck or nibble at your fingers as they touch the muzzle. Do not permit this. This is lesson number one in teaching a horse that fingers and other appendages are off limits to any kind of nibbling. You certainly don't want to discipline the foal for seeking to suck or nibble. Merely keep fingers out of its mouth.

Time to work on another building block — the legs. First, rub your hands up and down the legs in gentle, caressing fashion. The initial goal is to acquaint the foal with your touch, letting it know that this is just another gentle caress. When it accepts touching and rubbing of the legs and remains relaxed, it is time to quietly lift one of the forelegs.

The first time you pick up a foot, you very well might elicit a fear response. Nature gave the horse four strong legs on which it could flee from predators. Anything that compromises the horse's ability to run from danger can create fear, even in a day-old foal. When one of a horse's feet is lifted from the ground, its ability to run has been severely compromised and it might fight to free the leg.

If a foal fights to free its leg the first time you attempt to pick up a foot, don't fight to hang on. However, do not let the youngster escape the confinement of your arms. Having the foal's rump in a corner effectively blocks that avenue of escape while an arm across the chest prevents it from going forward. If the foal pulls a leg free, wait only a brief moment before picking it up again, after first rubbing your hand gently down the shoulder and the full length of the leg.

In most cases, the foal will quickly learn that having a foot picked up is not unpleasant.

There are, however, exceptions to every rule. Some foals will strongly resist. It is here that proper timing is important. The handler must recognize when the foal is beginning to establish an escape response that is getting more deter-mined each time an effort is made to pick up a foot.

When that occurs, it is time for the handler to assert his

Adapt training techniques to the individual.

or her dominance in the youngster's life for the first time. Gently maneuver the foal into a corner with a wall behind and on one side. Then with an arm across the chest to stop forward movement and using your body as another barrier, slowly and quietly pick up the nearest forefoot. This time when the foal seeks to pull it free, do not permit it. Hold the foot off the ground for only a second or two after the foal ceases struggling and then let it down. Repeat this process over and over until the foal realizes two things: first, that no harm will befall it if it allows its foot to be picked up, and second, that it must yield in its desire to pull the foot free of your grasp.

When you are able to pick up all four feet while the foal stands quietly, you are well on your way to establishing another building block that will make the young animal a farrier's delight instead of nightmare.

DAILY TRAINING SESSIONS

During the first week to 10 days of the young animal's life, go through this entire handling process on a daily basis. By the end of a week, the foal normally welcomes the attention and will follow you around the stall or paddock.

An important thing to remember at this stage and through the youngster's formative years is that a foal has a very limited attention span. Don't expect it to remain standing quietly while a foot is held aloft for long minutes on end. The foot should be held aloft for moments instead of minutes.

As the foal gets older, it will be time to hold the foot aloft for a longer period during the teaching session and to add other dimensions, such as cleaning the hoof with a hoofpick and gently tapping on the sole with a light wooden object as part of the preparation for one day nailing on a shoe.

During the first days of a foal's life, we also will want to prepare it for being saddled when older. As part of the rubbing and caressing, run your hand along and around its belly — especially just behind the forelegs where the girth or cinch will go — desensitizing it to touch in all spots, including the genital area.

This is also the time to put both arms around the foal just behind the withers, scratching and caressing wherever the fingers are touching it. We use our arms around its middle at the girth area to apply gentle pressure. This building block might well eliminate any battle later in life when a saddle is placed on the horse's back the first time and the cinch tightened.

The goal at this point is for the foal to accept being touched all over. You should be able to lift its tail without having it clamp it down tightly. You should be able to fondle the ears and poll without having the foal flinch. You should be able to rub your hands over its eyes and nostrils and around the muzzle without eliciting a pull-back reaction. You should be able to pick up each of its feet without resistance. And, most importantly, you should have accomplished all of this with the youngster steadily gaining confidence, rather than learning to fear a human's approach.

Remember that horses are individuals. No timetable to training success is the same for any two of them. One foal might respond from day one and become a willing and compliant student. Another might resist attention and instruction at any level. A good handler adapts training techniques to meet each individual's needs. With one, progress might occur in hours. With another, it might take days. Don't hurry the process. Learn to understand the foal and proceed accordingly and patiently.

To help instill confidence in the foal, use a quiet, kind voice. When you are fondling and caressing the youngster, you also should be soothing it with your voice. It doesn't matter what you say, just as long as the tone is quiet, gentle, and consistent. The horse can't understand specific words, but it can learn to differentiate between sounds.

The goal is to accustom the youngster to the same gentle voice quality whenever the handler enters the stall or paddock and begins working with it.

One of the most important lessons a foal can learn is to lead. That training, too, is best done in the first day or two of its life. We will deal with halter training in the next chapter.

CHAPTER 2

Teaching the Foal to Lead

The very best time to teach a foal to lead is in the first hours after birth. At this point in its life, the foal will stick to its mother's side like glue.

You will need a helper to lead the mare for this teaching session. First, put a halter on the foal and attach a lead shank to it. Second, use a soft cotton rope as a combination butt and chest rope. Pass the rope around the foal's rump, over the back, and beneath the neck in figure eight fashion. Grip the ends of this rope in one hand at the foal's withers. What you now have is a rope around the rump to induce forward motion and a rope around the base of the neck to restrict forward movement if that becomes necessary.

If the foal refuses to budge, you can apply pressure with the portion of the rope that goes around the rump. If the foal tries to run off or leap forward, it can be stopped and controlled with the rope around the base of the neck. If you have only a lead shank attached to the halter and the foal leaps forward, you are left with two options: pull it around with the lead shank and risk injury to its delicate legs and neck, or turn it free.

Now for the leading lesson. Ask your helper to lead the mare around the paddock. The foal normally will follow its mother with very little pressure needed from you. If it does resist, simultaneously apply pressure with the butt rope and with a tug on the lead shank. After making a few turns around the paddock, it is time for a little solo work. Ask your helper to stop the mare. Then, apply light pressure on both the lead shank and the rump rope to get the youngster to take a step or two away from the mare. The moment it takes a step, release all pressure.

Be satisfied with only a few steps because the foal's attention span is very short at this point in its life, plus it has an intense desire to be glued to its mother's side for security. The best approach is to work with the foal three or four times per day in very brief sessions. Your goal should be to get the youngster to move forward with ever decreasing pressure on the butt rope, ultimately responding to just a light tug on the lead shank.

If several days elapse before the first halter training lesson, you will be faced with a far more independent student and one that will resist any pressure to go forward.

Task number one is to get the halter on. That might sound easy, but it can be difficult if the foal is aloof and flighty. The best approach involves a two-person operation. One handler first can restrain the foal in the aforementioned cradle. Once the

> ## AT A GLANCE
>
> - Putting a halter on a foal for the first time might take two people.
>
> - Expect resistance at first when teaching a foal to lead.
>
> - The basic tenet in any equine training procedure involves moving away from pressure.
>
> - It might take an hour or more before the foal is following you around the stall or paddock.

Raising the tail can help quiet the foal.

foal is brought to a standstill, slide one hand up the buttocks to the base of the tail. Take a firm grip at the tail base — it works best to have the palm of the hand against the underside of the animal's tail — and quickly, but gently, lift it until the tail is almost straight in the air. Do not apply force to the point that the tail is bent over the foal's back. This can damage vertebrae. An arm around the foal's neck and another hand holding the tail aloft will make the youngster stand quietly, its powers of flight and fight totally negated. Holding the tail aloft does not inflict pain.

There are a couple theories concerning the physiological effect elicited by raising the youngster's tail. It is believed by a number of equine experts that raising the tail puts pressure on nerves that signal the brain to release endorphins. The endorphins place the foal in something of a euphoric or tranquilized state.

As the foal stands quietly, the second handler has an opportunity to affix the halter.

There are many foal halters on the market and it doesn't really matter which type is used — nylon or leather. The good news, bad news story on nylon halters is that they are virtually unbreakable. The good news is that they are durable and even the most feisty of foals won't break one. The bad news is that if a nylon halter is left on a foal who gets a rear foot caught while scratching or becomes hung up on a solid object, the unbreakable halter could cause the foal's death.

The logical solution to these potential problems is never to allow a foal to run at liberty while wearing a halter unless it is under constant surveillance.

EXPECT INITIAL RESISTANCE

Before beginning the halter training session with a foal that is already several days old, the handlers should recognize that they will encounter resistance. Knowing this, the instruction area, whether it is a stall or a paddock, should be properly prepared. This means that there should be no protruding objects. There should be board fences and the ground surface should be soft and yielding.

Perhaps the best place to begin is in the foal's stall.

There are two basic approaches that can be employed when teaching a foal to lead. One involves applying pressure with the halter only and the other involves applying pressure with both a looped butt rope and the halter.

In my early years of training, I always opted for the combination of lead line and butt rope, but have since learned that the butt rope often is more hindrance than help other than with the foal that is only hours old.

We must understand at this point that the basic tenet in any equine training

Leading a foal with a butt rope.

procedure involves moving away from pressure. Pressure is applied in many forms. A rider, for example, squeezes with the legs to get a horse to go forward. When you lead a horse forward or back it, pressure is applied either with a pull or a push and the horse is expected to respond accordingly. When a rider is moving forward on a horse and wants it to stop, pressure is applied on the bit and with a sinking of the body deeper into the saddle. As training advances, we can learn to turn a horse to left or right with slight pressure of the leg.

However, it all has to start somewhere and that somewhere involves applying pressure on the halter to get a foal to move forward. As mentioned, there is one constant in this teaching approach. Almost all foals will resist this form of pressure and fight against it. The handler's challenge involves applying the pressure consistently and staying with the project until success has been achieved. The approach to this type of training must be that the handler has all day to get the job done. If a time segment has been allotted for teaching the youngster to lead, failure will more often than not be the result.

The approach is both simple and complex. The simple part involves attaching a lead line to the foal's halter and applying

Make sure the lead line has a safety catch.

gentle pressure that asks the foal to move forward. The complexity involves timing and concentration. When a foal responds favorably, the handler has a split second to release the pressure so that the foal feels rewarded. This approach requires a great deal of patience; there is no room for anger or lapsed concentration. The lesson might last for 10 or 15 minutes, or it might go on for an hour. It all depends on the foal's personality and the handler's reactions.

Back to the simple part. Once the halter has been placed on the foal, the second handler steps aside. The handler on the lead line steps back, allowing five or six feet between his or her body and that of the foal. This provides the foal with space in which to move forward without being intimidated by the handler's close proximity. Gentle pressure is applied to the lead line. The degree of pressure applied is highly important. The goal is to avoid pulling the foal around. That is almost impossible. If too much pressure is applied, the foal will fight furiously and might flip over backwards.

Instead, we apply just enough pressure to induce an element of minor discomfort. During the first few minutes of the application of pressure, the foal normally will avoid it by pulling backwards. This is a key time. Don't try to stop the foal from moving backward. Let it move backward as much as it desires. However, as you walk forward with the backward-moving foal, do not relax the pressure. Let the foal move back as much as it pleases, but maintain constant and even pressure on the lead line.

When the foal comes to a halt, maintain the same pressure — no less, no more. The only time pressure is relaxed is when the foal seeks to rear in an effort to free itself or begins sinking to the floor to lie down. Again, timing is important. Try to anticipate what the foal will do before it has a chance to do it. The moment you anticipate a rear, release all pressure. If you maintain pressure when the foal rears, it might keep on pulling and tip over backwards.

The instant the foal is squared up again, immediately apply pressure. To increase the pressure without pulling harder, step to one side or another and continue applying pressure. This will put the foal slightly off balance and will encourage it to take a step forward to regain its balance. The very moment it makes even the slightest forward motion, release all pressure and use a calm, gentle voice to praise the foal.

Out in the paddock, you can get an extra edge by having someone lead the foal's dam to the other side of the paddock. The foal's natural inclination is to go to its dam for support and shelter.

A word of caution: The foal eventually will get tired of the constant pressure and move away from it. This means that the youngster will go forward. What you don't know is how it will move forward. With some it is a tentative step and then a halt. With others it might be a gargantuan leap that can cover the distance between you and the foal. Stay alert.

Whatever form the forward movement takes, the handler must be ready. Whether it is a step or a jump, release all pressure the moment the foal moves forward and praise it generously. Step to it and scratch it on the withers and over the croup. You know you are approaching success when the youngster relaxes its jaw and begins licking its lips. This is the foal's way of telling you that its stubbornness might remain intact for a while, but there is no fear.

After praising and petting the youngster, apply the pressure once again. Expect gaps in the progress. The foal might take several steps at a time, then sully up and plant all four feet. Patience. Continue the pressure. Release it the moment there is any forward motion.

Before long, a slight tug on the lead line will elicit a step or two forward and following shortly thereafter will be several more steps between tugs. The goal of the first session should be for the handler to make a circle of the paddock or spacious stall with the foal walking along in response to only light tugs on the lead line.

Do not expect super quick results with this method. It might take an hour or longer before the foal is following you around the stall or paddock. However, once a foal learns to lead this way, you will have cemented a building block that perhaps will be the most important in the horse's life.

First, the foal will have learned to yield to pressure. Second, you have established yourself as number one in that young animal's equine pecking order. The foal will have learned that it must yield space when you ask. The important thing is that you have taught this valuable lesson without dragging the foal around or by punishing it with a whip. All you have done is apply pressure and allowed the youngster to move away from that pressure.

I believe that using a butt rope at this stage only prolongs the learning process. Many times a foal will give to the pressure of the butt rope, but still will resist pressure on the halter. Thus, you might have a foal that will lead well as long as the butt rope is in place, but will put on the brakes when it is removed and pressure is applied only to the halter.

You will be amazed at the foal's retentive ability when you seek to lead it the second day. The youngster might plant all four feet a time or two, but normally that will last only for a few moments. If daily lessons using this method are continued for a week, the result will be a foal that will allow you to lead it most anywhere, even into scary places such as the inside of a trailer later in life. It will have become so ingrained in the animal's mind that it must move forward in response to pressure that it will rarely resist.

This approach also means that there rarely will be a problem when the foal is tied to a solid object for the first time. It will know that it must yield to pressure, so when it backs up and the object to which it is tied doesn't yield, the foal will. It merely will step forward to relieve the pressure. Thus, you are training it to be tied while training it to lead.

CHAPTER 3

Health Concerns

It is time to pause in our discussion of training methods and digress to health concerns of the young foal which can have a profound effect on the training approach.

The very first step in determining the foal's health status should be immediately after birth. Unless you are experienced in dealing with young foals, the best thing to do is call your veterinarian. He or she can examine the foal and tell you whether it is normal in all respects or has some abnormalities.

Among the most common abnormalities are legs or feet that appear to be deformed. Some abnormalities are normal, such as minor crookedness of the limbs. Time — a week or so — usually heals the problem.

Other foals have a more severe problem that might require corrective measures. Early training, in these cases, should be put on the back burner.

Most of the problems for the newborn involve either flexural or angular limb deformities, and a veterinarian should make the diagnosis in all cases. Flexural, as the term implies, involves the part of the leg that flexes. These deformities are observed when viewing the foal from the side. Angular deformities involve deviations that are seen when looking at the leg head on.

Many horse owners categorize all flexural limb deformities as "contracted tendons," though some experts, such as Dr. Gayle Trotter of Colorado State University, tell us that "true tendon contracture is unlikely the cause of the problem. The true cause and development of flexural deformities remains unknown…"

There are two types of deformities within both the flexural and angular category: those with which the foal is born (congenital) and those that develop after birth (acquired).

AT A GLANCE
• Most problems for the newborn foal involve either flexural or angular limb deformities.
• Flexural deformities also can occur in fast-growing young horses.
• Epiphysitis is an inflammation at the growth plates of a horse's long bones.
• Many factors can be involved in limb deformities, including genetics.

Many factors can be involved in congenital deformities, such as improper intra-uterine positioning, ingestion of certain toxins by the mare, and genetic predisposition. In some cases, multiple factors are involved.

Following are some of the flexural deformities that can occur, along with some of Trotter's recommendations for treatment:

DIGITAL HYPERTENSION

This condition occurs when a foal is born with very weak flexor tendons. When the foal stands or attempts to walk, its fetlocks will drop slightly or actually touch the ground. If the deformity is minor, correction usually will occur within two weeks as tendon tone improves. The strengthening period would not be a good time to teach the foal to lead. Instead, all training should be of a quiet nature, with the foal being held and stroked. About all of the training you want to do at this stage is to teach the foal to have its feet picked up and to get it accustomed to wearing a halter.

In severe cases, the foal might be walking on the bulbs of

the heel or pastern. The danger when the condition is severe is that the foal might suffer soft tissue abrasion injuries. Temporary heel extensions may be needed until tendon tone improves.

RUPTURED COMMON DIGITAL EXTENSOR TENDON

Affected foals will have swellings over the tendon sheath and at the outside of the knee. Foals also might appear a bit bowlegged and knuckle over at the fetlock when walking. They will appear to be over at the knee when standing. Application of a temporary splint to prevent knuckling over usually solves the problem.

This, too, is a condition that postpones normal halter training, although you should still give the foal plenty of attention. The danger, however, is that you will feel sorry for the youngster and allow it to develop bad habits, such as nibbling and biting, that will be difficult to correct later. Be kind to the foal, but do not baby it.

CONGENITAL KNEE DEFORMITIES

These deformities, when severe, can compromise the youngster's ability to develop normally. In less severe cases, temporary splinting often solves the problem.

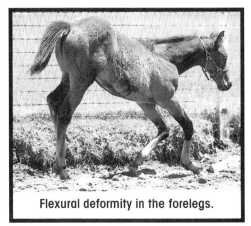
Flexural deformity in the forelegs.

CONGENITAL DEFORMITIES OF FOOT AND FETLOCK

Affected foals either will stand on the toe, or knuckle forward at the level of the fetlock. If the foal can stand and the limbs can be extended manually into a normal position, chances are that splinting will be able to correct the problem. Some cases might require surgery in the form of a check ligament desmotomy. Drug therapy is also an option.

ACQUIRED FLEXURAL DEFORMITIES

Next we turn to flexural limb deformities that develop during the first year or two of the foal's life. There are many things that can cause flexural deformities during the young horse's growing years, with nutrition often being implicated.

It has been found, for example, that flexural deformities seem to occur most commonly in fast-growing individuals who are on a high plane of nutrition. It also has been found that flexural deformities frequently occur when a malnourished foal is suddenly placed on a diet that involves plenty of good quality feed. Pain also can be a factor. If the foal is suffering from joint infection, physitis (pain caused by abnormal activity in the growth plate), or some other malady, it might alter its stance to alleviate the pain and a flexural deformity could result.

The acquired deformities tend to be manifested in two age groups. Deformities involving the coffin joint seem to develop in foals which are one to four months of age while deformities of the fetlock joint, when they occur, manifest in young horses 12 to 14 months of age.

Foals that develop a deformity at the coffin joint will have varying degrees of a more upright or clubbed foot appearance. In less severely affected foals, the front of the hoof wall will develop a dished appearance. Severely afflicted foals almost literally will be walking on the toe, with the heel not touching the ground.

One of the first steps to take is to evaluate the animal's diet. This usually results in limiting the foal's food intake. For nursing foals, it might mean separating mother and foal for periods of time to limit milk consumption.

Training of the foal during recovery from a coffin joint deformity should be very light. The youngster should be permitted only controlled exercise. If the problem is not severe, a specially designed glue-on shoe or device might be all that is needed. In more severe cases, a check ligament desmotomy might be required.

The young horse suffering from acquired flexural deformity of the fetlock joint will have an upright conformation in the front legs. When the problem is severe, there will be a knuckling forward at the fetlock joint. Young horses which develop fetlock deformity usually are in the 10- to 18-month age range. Horses which appear to be undergoing very rapid bone growth usually are afflicted. Again, diet is often implicated, so the first line of attack is to cut back on food intake.

If changing the diet doesn't solve the problem, corrective shoeing could be required, and surgery in very severe cases. Again, during the recuperation period, training other than very light exercise should be curtailed.

ANGULAR LIMB DEFORMITIES

Now let's take a look at angular limb deformities. This a condition in which there is deviation either outwardly (lateral) or inwardly (medial) at the knee, hock, or fetlock joints.

Angular limb deformities can result from numerous factors. As with flexural deformities, a foal might be born with the problem; or it might be incurred during early growth. Treatment varies, depending on the severity. Conservative therapy involves rest and corrective trimming and shoeing. Surgery might be required for the more severely afflicted.

When a foal is undergoing either form of therapy, all training procedures should be halted until the condition is rectified. Continued exercise of a limb with angular deformity can cause compression of the growth plate, and too much compression actually can impede growth. Surgical repair can take several forms, including periosteal stripping and transphyseal bridging.

EPIPHYSITIS

Another condition that can have an effect on how we train the young foal is epiphysitis. This, too, is a complex affliction that involves inflammation at the growth plates of the horse's long bones, such as the cannon bones, radius, and tibia.

These long bones develop from cartilage through a process known as endochondral ossification. Ossification means the formation of bone. The area at the end of the long bones where growth occurs is the growth plate. The growth plate consists of a cartilaginous portion, a bony portion, and the fibrous component that surrounds the periphery of the growth plate.

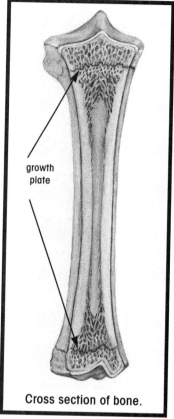

growth plate

Cross section of bone.

Eventually, the growth plate closes as the long bones reach their maximum length. Generally speaking, the growth plates at the lower extremities, such as the cannon bone, will close first while those at the knee and hock will close later in the young horse's development.

One of the first signs of epiphysitis will be swelling at the knee, ankle, or hock area. The swelling likely will be warm and the area will be sensitive to touch. Putting pressure on the area with one's fingers might cause the horse to move away. Frequently, the pain will be so intense that the horse will be lame.

When the above-described swelling and tenderness are observed, any training program should be halted. When a horse is in pain, it is incapable of learning. Its entire goal at this point is to find ways to alleviate the distress.

Epiphysitis seems to attack at two levels of equine development. If the condition afflicts the ends of the cannon bones, it normally will be manifested when the youngster is four to six months of age. When the problem area is at the end of the radius or tibia, the young horse is usually 12 to 20 months of age.

It is at these ages that physeal closure of the long bone growth plates tends to occur — four to six months of age for closure at the bottom of the cannon bones and 12 to 20 months for the bottom of the tibia and radius.

Once again, diet often is implicated. Overfeeding usually is the root problem, but malnourishment can be a cause as

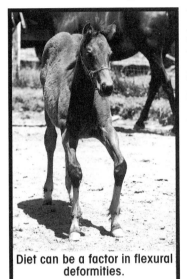

Diet can be a factor in flexural deformities.

well. The first step in a treatment program often involves cutting back on the amount of food energy the horse is ingesting or, in the case of the malnourished horse, slowly and steadily increasing its food quality and intake level. In some cases, with the overfed horse, a diet change might involve the elimination of all grain, with the horse being put on a grass hay or alfalfa/grass hay mix.

While a diet heavily laden with grain often is the culprit in the overfed horse, rich alfalfa hay also can contribute. Cases have been reported in which epiphysitis has developed in foals being fed third cutting alfalfa hay with no grain supplement.

Another culprit is the unbalanced diet, especially those lacking in calcium and phosphorous. A balanced diet is a must in the young, growing horse.

Stall rest might be required, but you want to achieve a proper balance of rest and exercise. Vigorous exercise can exacerbate the condition, but no exercise at all also can hurt. The problem with vigorous exercise is that it can result in continued trauma to the growth plate and might lead to permanent damage. The exercise, as recommended by a veterinarian, should be on a soft and yielding surface. Hopefully, a foal at this stage of life has been taught to lead. This means that exercise, as the pain level fades, also can be a learning experience as we work with the foal to travel correctly on the lead line during exercise sessions.

Phenylbutazone, also known as Bute, has been advocated by some researchers and practitioners to help alleviate epiphysitis pain and inflammation. However, too much Bute over a long period carries with it the risk of ulcers.

Many factors can be involved in limb deformities, including genetics. A mare which consistently gives birth to foals with deformities or a stallion which sires crooked offspring usually are passing along these traits.

Deformities can have a profound effect on the training program we envision for the young horse, as well as its future usefulness. It is far better to attempt to breed foals with sound, correct limbs. Even then, however, the battle isn't necessarily over. Proper diet and care during the developmental years are necessary to prevent acquired deformities.

CHAPTER 4

Weaning the Foal

Weaning is one of the most traumatic times in a young horse's life, but it is also an excellent time to establish more building blocks in the training program.

The first decision the owner must make is how to wean the foal. There are a number of theories that range from taking the foal from the mare for lengthening periods each day to the "cold turkey" approach in which dam and foal are separated suddenly and completely. Still others favor having dam and foal in adjacent paddocks where they can see, hear, and smell each other, but can't have physical contact such as nursing.

I favor the "cold turkey" approach for several reasons. First, both dam and foal have been inexorably moving toward separation during their final weeks of togetherness. The mare's milk supply has diminished and the foal has been depending more and more on grazing or eating hay and grain than on the mother's milk. The foal also has been moving toward a state of independence by straying farther away and for longer periods of time. The dam has been willing for that to happen. No longer does she nicker anxiously when the foal strays from her side. Instead, she merely continues grazing, lazing in the sun, or whatever.

It is also my opinion that it is easier on the mare physiologically. When there is complete separation from the foal, her milk production shuts down almost immediately. Her udder might become warm and firm the first day, but that will fade quickly. Manually milking her to relieve the pressure only prolongs the problem. Normally, the foal will be agitated for that first day, but if there is human contact, it will quickly forget about its dam.

The second weaning question involves whether to isolate the foal or put two or more in the same pen. It is best to keep newly weaned foals separated. By having a constant companion, a foal will bond with it just as tightly, or even more so, than it did with its dam. Then, when the time comes for separation, it is like going through the weaning process all over again.

AT A GLANCE

- In the "cold turkey" approach to weaning, mare and foal are suddenly and completely separated.

- The time to teach a young horse to accept being tied is after weaning.

- Hoof trimming is another important training building block.

- Begin teaching voice commands to the weanling.

Another consideration is that one of the foals might be much more aggressive than the other and be a source of constant and unhealthy intimidation.

Although not always possible, keeping foals in adjacent pens is the best of all worlds. They will have visual and audio contact with their peers, but not the kind of physical contact that promotes strong bonding.

How we approach adding more training building blocks depends on how much contact we have had with the foal during its pre-weaning days. A mare and foal that are brought into the barn every night results in daily contact with the foal. Such contact provides an excellent opportunity to cement the leading lessons. The wise approach during those weeks would be to catch the foal frequently, lead it about, tie it for the first time, and pick up its feet regularly.

However, if the foal and its dam roamed a large pasture

Early training can help in the weaning process.

during the pre-weaning period, you might face a foal which is shy of people and will need some review work with the basic building blocks, such as being haltered and led.

It is best to begin the review process before separating mare and foal. Return them to the box stall they occupied before being turned out. It will be familiar ground to both of them. With the mare providing a security blanket, the foal will be calmer than if separated and then approached by a handler.

If the early training has been handled correctly, the foal will return to the routine quickly. It might take a few minutes to get the youngster haltered. This should be handled slowly and quietly, with a lot of soothing words as you approach the foal. Once haltered, the foal should be led about the stall and then taken for a stroll away from its dam.

It might resist a time or two, just as it did some five or six months earlier when led for the first time. Use the exact same approach — merely apply firm, steady pressure with the lead shank until the youngster yields to pressure. Within minutes the foal should be following you about, just like it did during the early training sessions.

Decide where you are going to house the foal during the weaning period and allow it and its dam to spend a day and night there so that the area becomes home turf to the foal. The weaning stall or pen should be free of all protruding objects and plenty high so the foal isn't tempted to jump it. Many foals become quite agitated the first hour or two after the mare is removed, so stall or paddock safety is a high priority.

The first day or two after the mare and foal have been separated isn't a particularly good time for any type of serious training. Instead, it is a time to visit the stall or paddock frequently and pet and rub the foal, consoling it with a soft, soothing voice.

BUILDING BLOCKS FOR WEANLINGS

Once the foal, now a weanling, has settled into its new routine and no longer is calling mournfully for its dam, we can start with more building blocks. It is time to teach the weanling to accept being tied. Always tie to something immovable and make the tie above the youngster's head so that it can't become entangled in the rope.

Use a long rope for first-time tying so you can fashion a bow knot that you can quickly jerk free if the youngster gets into trouble. By using a long rope, you can walk around the animal and still have a hold on the rope end in case you quickly need to set the weanling free.

If the youngster has been taught to yield to pressure, it will be the rare one that fights being tied. It likely will pull back and make serious contact once and then give it up, already having been taught that resisting pressure is a losing cause.

FOOT CARE

If hoof trimming hasn't been necessary during the first five or six months of a foal's life, it very likely will be needed immediately after weaning. There is no magic time when a youngster's hooves should be trimmed the first time. They should be trimmed when trimming is needed, whether at several days of age or several months.

We can add an important building block here. Pick up and clean the feet with a hoof pick on a daily basis. When the youngster readily accepts this, add more dimensions. Use a light hammer or metallic object to tap on the hooves, simulating a farrier nailing on a shoe. Tapping the hoof should have been done when the foal was only a day or so old, but review sessions are important. Know the positions in which the farrier puts the legs during the various phases of trimming and shoeing and teach the weanling to allow its legs to be held in that manner.

Farriers use a number of tools during trimming and shoeing and all of them are noisy when dropped or banged about. The uninitiated weanling might become frightened when the rasp is dropped back into the tool box the first time. Prepare the foal for this by picking up and then noisily dropping objects while you are holding a foot aloft. Soon, the weanling will be desensitized to the movement and sound. You will have saved it from a good deal of trauma and you will be a hero in the eyes of your farrier.

RESPECTING PERSONAL SPACE

Weaning also is an excellent time to teach the youngster about yielding space to you. The only tool needed for this bit of education is a lead line attached to the halter. While holding the end of the lead line, begin backing up. The weanling will follow you because it has been taught to yield to pressure. By now, it should be yielding to "invisible" pressure. In other words, it should follow wherever you lead without ever tightening the lead shank. A slack lead shank is essential in carrying out the steps that follow.

It is time to teach the foal to stop when still a lead shank length from you. Come to a halt and give the lead shank a firm upward flick. This will jiggle the halter and the rope will ripple upward against the weanling's chin.

This is also a good time to begin teaching voice commands. As you give the upward flick, say, "Whoa" or "Hup" in a firm voice. If the weanling does not stop right away, step back from it and give another firm upward flick and repeat the command to halt. The moment the youngster stops, allow it to stand quietly with plenty of space between the two of you, with the lead shank drooping at the center.

Repeat the lesson until the weanling will come to a halt with only a slight flick of the lead shank. Once this lesson has been learned, it is time to add another dimension.

However, do not proceed to another building block until the "halt block" is firmly in place.

Still at the end of the lead shank, give a rolling flick and step toward the weanling, commanding it to "Back." The command to back should be in a different tone of voice than the "Whoa" or "Hup" to bring it to a stop.

Keep up with the rolling flicks until the weanling takes a step rearward. The moment it does, stop flicking the lead shank and verbally praise the youngster. Allow it to relax and then ask it to move backward again.

In only a couple sessions, the weanling should be halting on command with the slightest of flicks and should step backward spontaneously as you step forward.

We are returning to equine herd psychology here. In every group, there is a pecking order. Whenever a dominant horse approaches one lower in the order, the lesser horse will give up its space to the dominant one. As trainer, we are gently and quietly inserting ourselves into the role of "dominant horse" in the weanling's life. It is learning that we have control of its space and that it must yield to us. The beauty is that we are making this point without ever resorting to force.

There will be times when we don't want to be leading the horse at the end of the lead shank. We will be wanting to lead it while walking off the shoulder. Up to this point, the youngster has been following its handler and feeding off the handler in the way of security. It is comfortable knowing that it is walking in the tracks of a trusted human.

Now we will change that. We will ask the weanling to step forward with no one in front of it. Instead, we will be at its shoulder. If all of the foregoing steps have been successfully completed, this usually will be an easy transition. You merely reach forward with the right hand on the shank and provide pressure to move forward. The weanling might hesitate and even violate your space in its quest for security. This is the time to be gentle, but firm. Using a hand on the neck, push the youngster away, so there is space between the two of you, then repeat the forward pressure.

In rare cases, the weanling will decide not to go forward. Time to add another form of pressure and proper position-

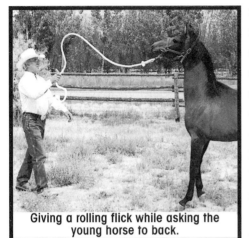

Giving a rolling flick while asking the young horse to back.

ing. The proper positioning means that there will be an obstacle on the weanling's right side, such as a corral fence, and something behind it so that it can't back. The corner of a corral is the ideal spot. The handler's body is the third barrier. Now there are barriers in every direction but forward. When this is the case, the weanling normally will take

the "escape route" and go forward. If it is particularly stubborn, we apply the next form of pressure. With the lead shank in the right hand, take a light whip in the left. Standing at the youngster's left shoulder and facing forward, reach back and gently tap it on the hocks with the whip. The only way to escape the new pressure is by going forward, and this the weanling will do.

DESENSITIZATION

An intermediate step sometimes is required before progressing to this new form of leading and even stopping and backing while on the lead shank as well as the picking up of feet. Weanlings come in all shapes and sizes and in a variety of personalities. Some are uncommonly jittery and jumpy, becoming frightened at all of our moves and touches, even though they are slow and deliberate.

When this is the case, it is the time for desensitizing. Again, no force is required. Tie a piece of plastic firmly to the end of a fairly stiff whip. Have the weanling on a lead shank in a relatively small space, such as a box stall. Gently start passing the noisy plastic along its body. Start at the withers and work

kicking in what it considers self-defense, you should undertake a quiet, steady course of action. Make certain that you stay out of range of those back feet and work a good deal with the youngster in building confidence. Be firm, but gentle in making it yield space while being led, for example.

After gaining the horse's confidence on the front end, it is time to switch to the rear. With the horse either tied or the lead shank in your hand, stroke it along the back, over the croup, down the buttocks and past the hocks. Always stay close against the horse's side so that if it does kick, you are not a target.

If this approach does not work despite repeated attempts on your part, it is time to get a little tougher. With the young horse tied securely, stand at its side and pass a light broomstick or cane down the rump, over the

Using a broom handle to discourage kicking.

hock and on down the leg. Hold it in such a position that when the young horse lashes out, it will strike the side of the cannon bone against the broom handle. This will produce a stinging sensation, but will not injure the horse. If you use a heavy piece of material, there is danger of injury — thus, the light broom handle.

Be very calm and patient. Let the horse punish itself. In the horse's mind, you become only a bystander because you are not raising an aggressive hand against it. Eventually, the youngster will get tired of stinging itself each time it kicks. When you are able to rub the broom handle up and down the leg without eliciting a negative response, go to the other rear leg and do the same thing. Slowly, but surely, it will dawn on the young horse that kicking results in a painful experience.

The more aggressive approach involves the use of a whip and is appropriate for the young horse that kicks out when it becomes irritated at, for example, having been asked to yield its leg. Again, make certain that you understand why the animal is kicking. Is there a way to solve the problem by removing a negative stimulus?

When other options have been exhausted, take a light flexible whip in hand. Keeping yourself out of danger, maneuver the youngster into a position where it will be inspired to lash out. The moment it does so, give it one very sharp crack across the hocks with the whip. Two things are important here. The first is timing. The sting of the whip must be felt while the young horse is in the process of kicking in order for it to associate discipline with negative behavior. Equally important is that you give it one crack with the whip and one only, when it kicks. We are not aiming to beat something out of the young horse. We are merely serving up discipline in response to negative action.

Follow the discipline with pets and soft, quiet words. We are still the young horse's friend, but by lashing out with a foot it has violated the "dominant horse's" space. Again, we are drawing on herd psychology. If a young horse lashed out at the dominant horse in a band, there would be instant and painful retribution. The handler has become the dominant figure in the young horse's life and must act accordingly.

Dealing with a young horse that strikes with a front foot is more dangerous, but involves the same approach. Again, the important thing from a handler safety viewpoint is to stand close beside the horse so that you are always out of range.

LEARNING TO STAND QUIETLY

Another irritating habit a young horse can develop is being fidgety while tied for longer than a few minutes. This is another vice that is far easier to prevent than to cure. Once the youngster has been tied and has learned that pulling back is not an option, we can work on getting it to stand quietly for lengthening periods.

First of all, don't tie it in the dark corner of a box stall and expect it to stand there patiently. Tie it in an area where there is other activity going on, such as horses coming and going or people moving about. You don't want the young horse in the midst of the activity. Instead, the horse should be tied in a tranquil spot from where the activity can be viewed.

Leave the horse unattended for only a few minutes the first time. Then return and do something constructive, such as picking up and cleaning a foot. Gradually lengthen the sessions when the horse is alone until it will stand quietly for up to an hour. It is important that at the end of these sessions, you don't reward the young horse with grain or treats. By so doing, you will have negated all the positive things achieved during the tying session. The horse quickly

Teaching a youngster to stand quietly.

will equate treats with being untied and will impatiently await that moment. Instead of treats, end a session with grooming, including picking up and cleaning the feet and combing out mane and tail.

If you purchase a young horse that will not stand quietly while tied, it can take many sessions to solve the problem. Start in the same way as described above by tying the horse where it can observe other activity, but is not in the midst of it. We must watch for a positive reaction on the horse's part and respond quickly. If the horse stands quietly for a few minutes, untie it. Make the next session last for an additional several minutes. Never end a session when the horse is pawing or moving about as the act of untying will only reward its behavior. It also is of no use to discipline the horse. Giving it a crack with the whip will only increase its agitation.

If you fail to get positive results when the horse is tied in sight of activity, you might conclude that this is part of the problem. You might try an opposite approach. Take the horse out of sight and sound of humans and other horses and tie it securely. Follow the same protocol. Untie and remove the horse only after it has remained standing quietly for a time.

Make certain the lead shank is short enough and is tied high enough that the horse can't get a front leg over it if the youngster should begin pawing or striking. A good approach is to use two lead shanks in a modified cross tie. Each will go to its tying spot in diagonal fashion in front of the youngster instead of directly to the side. This way the horse is prevented from completely turning its body into the fence or hitching rail, but still is allowed some freedom of movement. In the West, this is called "soaking."

In a worst case scenario, you might have to leave a horse "soaking" for a long period of time before it finally gives up and stands quietly. If the horse is not shod, be certain that you tie it on soft ground rather than hard earth or concrete. If the animal begins pawing, packed earth or other equally hard surfaces can cause hoof damage. A session should end only after the horse has remained standing quietly for a period of time.

RESPECTING SPACE

Still another vice that must be dealt with immediately when it arises is violation of the handler's space. If you have followed the procedures discussed during early leading sessions, this problem should not arise. But, again, it can be a major problem when you buy a horse that someone else has trained or, more likely, not trained.

This is the horse that shoulders into you when you lead it and doesn't mind in the least if its hoof lands on your foot.

It is a problem that normally can be solved in non-aggressive fashion. You will likely need an aid in addition to just using your hand to push the horse away. Start by using your hand against the horse's neck, but be ready to move immediately to the next step. If the horse pushes through your hand, take the lead shank in one hand and hold a hard, blunt object in the other. The butt end of a short whip works well. Make certain that the object has no sharp edges and that it does not have a sharp point.

Hold the butt end of the whip a couple inches from the horse's neck and lead it forward with the other hand. As it attempts to move toward you, hold the whip firmly in place so that it presses into the animal's neck. The horse will be the one applying pressure against itself and it quickly will learn that this is unpleasant. Very soon, the horse will realize that if it maintains space between the two of you, the pressure will not exist.

If the young horse is persistent in violating your space, apply the pressure in an area that is far more sensitive than the neck. This is just behind the jowl at the hinge of head and neck. Never jab or push hard. Instead, let the horse apply the pressure. You merely hold the restraining object in place.

When the horse no longer pushes against the butt of the whip, you are well on the way to victory. It is important that you not pet and praise the horse when it responds positively while being led. That could serve as an invitation to move back in for more praise and loving. Wait until you bring the horse to a halt and then pet it. Repeat the sessions until the horse has a clear understanding of where your space begins.

CHAPTER 6
Teaching Voice Commands

In this chapter, we have combined a discussion on the training of yearlings and two-year-olds because the same approaches will apply to each age group. Just when we do what with the young horse at this stage of its life depends on its rate of physical development and mental maturity.

In some breeds, such as the Thoroughbred, race training begins when the young horse is a long yearling. Normally, its birth comes early in the year and by the time fall of its yearling year rolls around, the "yearling" is nearing two years of age chronologically. The universal birth date for all Thoroughbreds is January 1.

With non-racing breeds, there is more latitude in when to begin a particular training regimen. If we are astute horsemen, we will let the young horse tell us when it is ready for training under saddle, rather than make the decision based on the calendar.

Everything should depend on development. At the risk of sounding contradictory, it should be said that some young horses are started in formal training too early because they haven't reached an appropriate state of physical maturity while other horses are started too soon because they are maturing too rapidly.

In other words, the underdeveloped horse simply isn't

This foal is 2½ months old and being taught to yield to pressure from the lead shank. The foal resists (1 & 2) — which is not unusual at first — and tries to get away (3).

The foal begins to yield to pressure (4), then
finally walks along in a responsive fashion (5).
I praise and pet the foal (6) at the end of the
training session.

During an early leading session, I use the blunt end of a whip (1) to prevent this 2-year-old filly from shouldering into me; I gently massage this yearling's poll (2) to get her to lower her head; I am using a plastic bag (3) to help desensitize her.

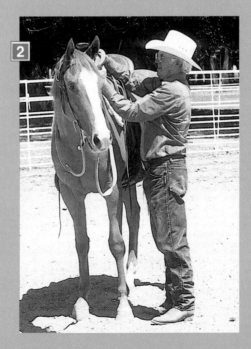

I secure the stirrups (1) and the reins (2) before I begin teaching this 2-year-old to drive in long lines.

I ask her to move forward at the walk (3), then ask her to bend (4) as I apply light pressure on the inside line; I bring her to a halt (5) with light contact on the bit and a voice command.

After making sure the cinch is tight, I prepare to mount. I encourage the filly to stand quietly as I prepare to swing my right leg over the saddle.

I ask the filly to walk off as I use a combination of leg
pressure and voice command. I then dismount from the
right side to prevent the filly from becoming one-sided.

Using English tack this time, I tighten the girth (1), then I make sure the filly is aware of me (2) as I quietly step aboard; I gently open my left hand (3) as I ask her to step out and to the left.

strong enough yet for the rigors of riding. On the other hand, the rapidly developing horse may have a large, muscular body, but insufficient leg and joint strength to carry that body with a rider aboard.

My rule of thumb is to start under saddle the horse whose body and legs are deemed ready in the spring of its two-year-old year. The lesser developed horse or the one which is out of balance in its development is left until the fall of the two-year-old year or, in some rare cases, spring of the three-year-old year. This, of course, is just a general guideline. Each horse is different and the decision on when to start riding it must remain an individual one.

AT A GLANCE

- The pre-riding weeks or months are a good time to teach more building blocks.

- Consistency is the key using verbal commands.

- A round pen is essential when training on a lunge line.

- Keep round pen sessions short to prevent undue pressure on a young horse's bones, tissues, and joints.

Even though the yearling may be too immature for riding, that doesn't mean we can't add more training building blocks. The pre-riding weeks or months are a good time to establish some more basics. During this time, you can teach the horse to wear a bit and saddle and learn how to turn to the left and right in response to pressure on the bit.

This also is a time when we can teach the young horse to respond to verbal commands. Yes, we can actually talk to horses if we understand what they can comprehend and what they can't.

A horse does not have the ability to differentiate between specific words, but it can comprehend changes in tone. It doesn't matter what words are used. It only matters how they are uttered. With the horse, consistency is the key. If we are to seek a response to voice commands, the exact same tone of voice must be used each time the command is given.

We already have mentioned using "Hup" or "Whoa" when we want the horse to stop and "Back" when we want it to back up. We can start our verbal response training by reviewing the command to stop.

By now, the horse should be leading off the shoulder, while giving the handler appropriate space at the end of the lead shank. Walk along at the horse's shoulder, and when you give

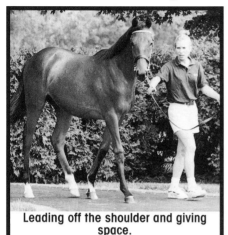

the "Whoa" command, do it in a firm voice with a single sharp syllable. Simultaneously, give a downward tug on the lead shank and come to a halt yourself. Repeat this with lighter and lighter tugs on the lead shank until the horse will stop with only the verbal command.

Leading off the shoulder and giving space.

The rest of the verbal commands are taught when the horse is on a 30-foot lunge line. At this point in the training, a round pen of some sort is essential. If you don't have a round pen, you can construct one with metal gates or panels. It is important that the surface of the round pen be yielding. You definitely do not want a rock-hard surface.

The other aid, in addition to a lunge line, is a lunge whip, 10 or 12 feet in length. The bottom half of the lunge whip consists of a stiff handle while the top half is a flexible lash. The important thing about a lunge whip is to understand that it is an aid, not an instrument for inflicting punishment. It will be used to apply a form of pressure from which the horse will move away.

The round pen should be small enough so that you can stand in the center and when the horse is against the outer extremity, it will not be at the end of the lunge line. If the round pen is too large, you will wind up playing tug of war with the horse, something you want to avoid.

To begin the first lesson, attach the lunge line to the halter and lead the horse to the center of the round pen. Fold the lash of the lunge whip back to the base of the handle. Step back and away from the horse. You should be positioned just behind the youngster's shoulder. Gently tap it on the buttocks or hocks with the folded lunge whip. The horse's first inclination will be to turn and step toward you, confusing the command with being led at the end of a lead shank.

At this point, continue stepping toward the horse's rear and away from the horse itself. Give another tap with the lunge whip. The moment the horse takes a legitimate step forward, be certain that all pressure on the lunge line is released. It won't be long before the horse will understand that it should move away from the pressure being applied at the rear. It is highly important that the horse be taught to move in a circle while traveling in both directions. Again, we are seeking to avoid a one-sided horse.

It should be pointed out that the horse's unique vision makes it imperative that the animal be taught from both sides. The horse's vision is both binocular and monocular. This means that when it looks at something in the distance, it focuses both eyes for binocular vision. However, because of the way the horse's eyes are located at the side of its head, it is also capable of monocular vision, or seeing and recording something with one eye only. This means that if something happens on its right side, it can record the image with its right eye only. The brain receives this signal from the right eye. When the horse is turned and records the same scene with the left eye, it is almost as though the brain is receiving a whole new signal.

It is for this reason that when a horse is ridden in an arena, for example, that it might be skittish when viewing activity on the rail with its right eye. Eventually, it will become desensitized, but when it is asked to traverse the arena in the opposite direction and records the same activity with the left eye, it might well become agitated all over again. Thus, it is essential in all phases of training that you work from both sides of the horse in equal measure.

Once the horse understands that it is to go forward at a walk and travel in a circle within the confines of the round pen, you can add another word to its vocabulary. Before doing so, however, make certain that it remembers the command to stop. When you want to effect a halt, give the "Whoa" command and simultaneously give a firm tug on the lunge line. Because the command to halt should bring an instant stop in forward movement, I insert a preparatory command when working on the lunge line. It serves to give the horse a second to prepare itself for the actual stop command.

I use the words "Easeeee. HUP!" The first word is long and drawn out while the "HUP" is a short, sharp sound. The first word, once its sound has become entrenched in the horse's mind, prepares it for the final command to cease forward movement.

I use the command "Hup" instead of "Whoa" because whoa is a little too much like the next command which also contains a 'W'. After the horse has halted and is standing quietly some distance from you, unfurl the lunge whip and tell it to "Waaalk" in a mild, drawn out, steady tone of voice. Simultaneously, flick the end of the lunge whip lightly against

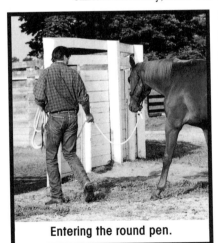
Entering the round pen.

the horse's hocks to provide pressure that tells it to once again move forward. If the horse becomes a bit exuberant and wants to break into a trot at this point, give a firm tug on the lunge line accompanied by repeated commands to "Waaalk."

Only after you have the horse walking around you both ways on command without being tapped with the lunge line and halting without so much as a tug, should you progress to the next word in the vocabulary. The new word is "Trot."

As the horse is moving forward at a walk in response to the verbal command, tell it to "TROT!" The single syllable word should be uttered in short, sharp fashion so that it does not sound at all like any of the other commands. The command to stop is also short and sharp, but with the "TROT" we have two T's that produce a different sound than the 'H' and the 'P' in "Hup."

The command should be accompanied by a flick of the lunge whip against the hocks. Once the horse is trotting both ways of the ring in response to verbal commands, you can use the commands in sequence. With the horse standing quietly, command it to "Waaalllk." Once it is doing so comfortably, urge it into the "TROT." After a couple circles, bring it back to the walk with a voice command, then give the halt command.

The next verbal command must be taught carefully. It is the command to move forward at a canter. It should be uttered as two distinct syllables, with the first syllable being longer — "CANNN-TER!"

Exactly when this particular command is taught in the round pen depends on the young horse's state of physical development. Earlier, we discussed bone growth and how the fragile bone centers can become inflamed. You can put serious stress on young joints

A horse has to learn to go forward and travel in a circle.

by having the horse travel at a canter in a tight circle. Only when you feel that the youngster's legs and joints have reached an appropriate level of maturity should the horse be asked to canter in a tight circle. Even the trotting in the round pen should be at an easy jog rather than a long, reaching trot.

When the verbal command to canter is taught, it always should be in transition from the trot. As the horse is trotting around you, give the command to "CANNN-TER," and accompany it with a flick of the lunge whip. Expect the horse to

A later round pen lesson under tack.

spend a little more time assimilating this command than the ones for halting, walking, and trotting. Moving from the two-beat trot to the three-beat canter or lope is a more difficult transition. The horse must learn to lead off correctly so that it remains balanced at the canter. This could take a bit of time with the awkward youngster, so be patient.

Once the horse gets the hang of cantering on voice command, work it through the entire vocabulary — from halt, to walk, to trot, to canter, and from canter down to trot and from there down to walk and finally, the halt.

The sessions in the round pen should be brief for two reasons. The first involves preventing undue pressure on bones, tendons, and joints while the horse travels in a circle. The second involves the young horse's attention span, which is quite short. Long sessions of going in a circle in the confines of an enclosed pen can quickly sour a horse and cause the animal to avoid learning instead of embracing it.

Always quit on a positive note. If you have asked the horse to do something new and you get a quick response, quit on the spot, even though the session may have lasted only five minutes. Then, begin the next day with a short review session that takes you to the previous day's stopping point and go forward from there.

However, if the horse is resisting unduly, you must stay the course until at least a partial positive response is obtained.

The key is to recognize what constitutes a positive response. This will vary horse by horse and can be comprehended by the trainer only if he or she concentrates on the horse and understands all of its little idiosyncrasies.

Once we have the horse responding to voice commands, it is time for saddle and bridle and a few sessions of driving in long lines before climbing aboard.

CHAPTER 7
Training Under Saddle

The next building blocks in the young horse's training regimen will be added in a natural progression and result in the horse working under saddle in a non-traumatic way.

We make the assumption at this point that the horse is properly developed physically and mentally to handle the rigors of being ridden.

While the steps that will be discussed in this chapter follow in logical order those taken to get the horse to respond to verbal commands on a lunge line, they do not necessarily have to follow in immediate sequence. There is nothing wrong with a break for the young horse in between the different, but ongoing, training segments. In fact, it is often beneficial.

The young horse will not forget what it has learned during the lay-off period. In fact, it will appear to have learned more. This process is referred to as latent learning. There will be, and have been, many instances in which a young horse seems to reach a wall in its learning process. No matter what you do, no progress is being made.

This is a time to give the horse a break. Turn it out for a month or so. You might be surprised at how responsive it has become when you resume the training regimen.

We must be as concerned with mental maturity as with

physical maturity when training the young horse. Some youngsters can absorb only so much and then just seem to check out mentally. These trainees need a break. Other horses that are more mentally mature can continue on in the training program without interruption.

If physical problems such as inflamed joints arise at any point in the training process, all vigorous training should come to a halt.

TIME FOR BIT AND SADDLE

Though the horse is responsive when working in the round pen, bear in mind that you are now going to introduce it to something new. Take your time and be patient.

Carry saddle, pad, and bridle to the round pen and place them in the center. Lead the horse to the equipment and let it sniff and nose them about. Next, while the horse is on the lunge line, quickly review all the voice commands.

Bring it back to the center. Pick up the pad and let the horse smell it. Rub the pad along the horse's neck and back, eventually settling it into place. Do the same with the saddle. Remember that although the horse has monocular vision that also allows it to look to the side and toward the rear, it can't look directly behind. Thus, when you place pad or saddle on the horse's back, it is unable to see those objects. For this reason, you rub the pad and saddle along the horse's neck and withers so there is an uninterrupted sensation of touch.

If you are using an English saddle, run the irons to the top of the leathers so they don't bang against the youngster's sides. With a western saddle, fold cinch and off stirrup over the seat of the saddle for the same reason while saddling.

Have a lead shank or the lunge line — the lead shank is

better because there is less chance of you becoming entangled — draped over your arm so that if the horse tries to move off, you can check it. If it takes a nervous step or two one way or the other, that's okay, but avoid having the saddle slide off and frighten the youngster.

If you are using a western saddle, settle it onto the young-

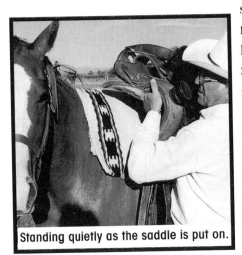

Standing quietly as the saddle is put on.

ster's back, then step around in front of the horse and quietly lower the off stirrup and cinch. Step back to the other side and reach underneath the horse's belly for the cinch or girth. Tighten lightly and allow the youngster to get used to the feel of the strange object on its back and the sensation of pressure around its middle. A minute or so later, tighten cinch or girth a bit more. It is far better to tighten the cinch or girth several times, than to pull it tight in one abrupt move. If we are abrupt, the horse will resent the pressure and seek ways to avoid it, either by moving off or expanding its sides. Before beginning a training session under saddle, however, make certain that the cinch or girth is tight enough to prevent the saddle from slipping off to one side.

Next comes the bridle and bit. During the youngster's formative years, you should have been asking it to lower its head by gentle, massaging pressure on the sensitive poll. If you have done your homework, bridling will not be a chore. Simply hold the top of the bridle in your right hand and pass your right arm over the top of the horse's head between the ears. The familiar pressure on the poll will cause it to drop its head. Holding the snaffle bit in your left hand, gently insert a thumb or finger into the bar area of the mouth where there are no teeth. Exert enough pressure so that the horse opens it mouth. Quietly pull the bit upward with the right hand and put the bridle over the ears.

Proper fit of the bit is important. It should rest against the corners of the mouth, but should not be so tight that it creates a crinkle. The only bit appropriate at this stage of the horse's training is the snaffle — D-ring or loose ring. I prefer a D-ring that has rollers along the mouthpiece. Half of the rollers are copper, which are designed to increase salivating.

The rollers allow the horse to move its tongue back and forth easily on the bit and this also increases production of the lubricating saliva.

Time to let the young horse, now on a lunge line, walk off carrying its new burden. Using the voice commands, interspersed perhaps with clucking or

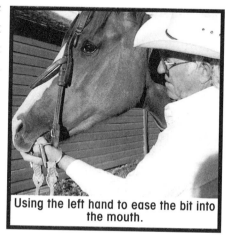

Using the left hand to ease the bit into the mouth.

kissing sounds, ask it to walk. Normally, the horse will take a few gingerly steps, then relax and travel as though nothing new has been added.

BUCKING

In some horses, the saddle arouses latent fears passed on by its ancestors. Horses always have been animals of prey and in the early days of the species' existence, many predators waited in tree branches above pathways. When the horse traveled beneath the tree, the predator dropped onto its back, digging in with sharp claws and biting into the neck with long teeth located in powerful jaws.

Thus, it is natural for a horse to want to rid itself of an object on its back and the way to do that is by bucking. There are two schools of thought as to how you should react if the young horse begins bucking when first saddled. Some feel that the horse should be allowed to buck all it desires so that it learns that the saddle can't be dislodged. Others feel that no bucking at all should be tolerated and that the horse should immediately be brought to a halt and started over.

I operate somewhere between the two. I allow the horse a few experimental jumps or hops and then don't allow it to buck any more. The horse has a right to react to the foreign object in its own way, but it must learn quickly that bucking is not an option. Here is where the verbal commands are so important. You can slow the horse or bring it to a halt with your voice instead of using heavy force on the lunge line.

Once the horse relaxes, put it through the entire vocabulary of verbal commands while traveling on the lunge line and carrying saddle and bridle. Go through this same procedure for a couple of sessions, until you feel the horse has accepted both bit and bridle. It will tell you that the bit is no longer a bother by carrying it quietly without trying to chew on it or opening its mouth.

When the horse has accepted the bit, it is time for it to learn about rein pressure. I always use a western saddle for the next sequence of building blocks. Attach a light rope to the bit and tie the other end in a bow knot to the rear D-ring of the saddle. You want just enough pressure on the bit so that the horse will find relief from the pressure if it turns its head in that direction.

Once again, still using the lunge line, direct it around the round pen on voice commands. Do not ask it to canter at this point as this will put undue pressure on the mouth of the uncoordinated horse. Instead, start at a walk and when that has been handled calmly and confidently both ways, ask for the trot.

It will take a couple training sessions to get the horse to yield to the bit pressure. For each session, put just a little more pressure on the bit, so that the horse learns that it must bend neck and body to gain relief.

If the horse is unresponsive, you might need longer sessions with the horse learning on its own. Bit it around as described and then unfasten the lunge line and allow it to move about at will. The horse will soon learn that giving in to the pressure is much easier than fighting it.

Once you are getting positive response to bit pressure, it is time for driving in long lines. Simply hobble the stirrups by passing a light rope from one to the other beneath the horse's belly and securing it. Run a lunge line through each stirrup and attach to the bit. The line running through the left stirrup attaches to the left ring of the snaffle, and the line running through the right stirrup attaches to the right side. Give the verbal command to walk and at the same time apply light pressure with one driving line or the other. By tugging on the left line, while giving the verbal command to walk, for example, you will be adding extra encouragement for the student to take that first step. If the horse is still hesitant to respond, use the lash of the lunge whip to give it a light flick around the hocks.

As the horse travels around the ring, begin directing it with the lines. Once it responds to pressure on the bit, ask it to reverse direction by applying pressure with the outside line. The line will pass along the horse's body and between its buttocks and hocks, providing you with the necessary leverage.

Next, ask the horse to stop by using a combination of verbal command and left-right tugs on the lunge lines. Never pull back with both hands simultaneously. This will encourage the horse to resist the pressure.

It won't be long before the horse will be doing figure eights at the walk and trot, in response to only light pressure on the bit and stopping on voice command with only light tugs.

RIDING THE HORSE

Once this part of the training is going along in good order, it is time for the climactic event — riding the horse for the first time. With all of the building blocks in place, however, riding is only another logical step in the sequence, and should be more anti-climactic than climactic.

Before climbing aboard the first time, you should have done some preparatory desensitizing. If the horse is jittery and excitable, it is a good idea to get it accustomed to seeing an object looming above its head. Climb to the top corral rail or board and use the lead shank to bring the horse toward you, reaching down to pet it and rub its head.

After it has accepted the saddle, prepare it for movement and sound. Grasp a stirrup and slap the fender or leather up and down against the horse's side. Get it used to bracing against weight by pulling against the saddle horn or pommel and by stepping up and down in the stirrup.

When the horse has accepted all of the above, getting on the first time is not a traumatic event. If the horse to be mounted appears apprehensive, have a halter on beneath the bridle. When you are ready to mount, grasp the halter in your left hand and pull the horse's head around so that it can see what you are doing. Then, with right hand on the saddle horn or pommel, swing up and settle quietly into the saddle. Release your grip on the halter and stroke the horse on the neck, speaking to it in a quiet, soothing voice.

Step off and go to the other side. Using the same procedure, swing up again. Mount and dismount until the horse shows no signs of stress. When you hear it let out a sigh and it begins licking its lips, you will know that it is relaxed.

Swing into the saddle again and this time apply a bit of direct rein pressure on the bit, asking the horse to turn left or right. At the same time give it the verbal command to walk. If the horse resists, use the end of the reins or a short riding whip that you are carrying to give it a light tap on the rear.

The horse will remember instantly that it has learned to move away from lunge whip pressure and will walk off. Expect it to be unbalanced and uncoordinated during those initial steps, but it will come around quickly and soon you will be giving the verbal command to trot.

Your most important role at this point is to be relaxed and confident. Horses are extremely sensitive and if the rider is uptight, this will be transmitted to the horse as clearly as human messages are transmitted along telephone lines. Remember who you are in the horse's mind. You are the dominant member of its "band." You are in the role of lead horse and your young charge wants to trust you and have confidence in you. You have become its security blanket. To play your role properly, remember this and remain calm, relaxed, and confident.

If you are relaxed and confident, the horse will be relaxed and confident. If you are tense and apprehensive, the horse will be tense and apprehensive.

The most important thing a horse can learn when being ridden is to stop on command. Work on this from the first session on, combining a voice command with a settling of weight in the

Preparing to mount for the first time.

saddle and light pressure on the bit. You are building toward the horse that will come to a halt with only a slight lift of the rein hand or a settling of your weight in the saddle.

It is extremely rare that a horse which has been started in training as described thus far will buck. However, there are exceptions to every rule. If the horse should try to buck, abruptly pull its head around to your knee with force so that it is unable to get leverage and forward momentum. Bring it to a halt with a combination of a sharp verbal command and firm pressure on the reins, then start over again.

Once you are on the horse and have ridden it several times in the round pen, it is time to graduate to bigger and better things. The days in the round pen are over. It is time for some open spaces and more building blocks.

CHAPTER 8
Riding the Horse

The next training building blocks are perhaps the most enjoyable. You are going to be riding the young horse on a regular basis. One of the most satisfying accomplishments for a trainer is to feel the young horse grow and develop under his or her tutelage, becoming ever more confident and relaxed with each outing.

It is important that you do not spend more than a couple sessions riding in the round pen. Its purpose was to allow you to do the basic training work in a confined area where it was easy and natural for you to be in control. To continue riding in that confined space, once the horse has accepted saddle, bit, and you, would be counter-productive. The horse soon would get bored traveling around in a small circle and its learning capability would diminish as its rate of boredom advanced. It is time now to graduate to a larger arena or to the open spaces of cross country trails.

Riding into the open.

I feel that the best next step is trail riding. There is nothing wrong with riding in a large arena, especially if trail riding areas are limited, but that type of riding does not broaden the horse's learning horizons quite as much nor as quickly. When you take to the trails the first time, be sure that another rider accompanies you and is mounted on a trusted trail horse.

You can take it a step further. On that first ride, lead the young horse from the back of a solid, calm trail horse. You should still be accompanied by another rider, also mounted on a totally trustworthy horse. Travel up hills and down and along level pathways until the young horse appears relaxed and confident.

> ## AT A GLANCE
>
> • Use trail riding as a way to teach the horse new lessons.
>
> • The first trail rides should be used to build the horse's confidence.
>
> • One of the biggest challenges for most young horses is wet ground.
>
> • Horses can develop the vice of refusing to stand while the rider mounts and dismounts.

At that point, dismount from the horse you are riding, turn it over to your fellow rider and get on the young horse. The accompanying rider then sets off leading the horse you had been riding. Allow the youngster to drop behind the horse it has been trailing so that it doesn't have to worry about what is in front of it. Normally, the young horse will follow in the footsteps of the horse in front without hesitation.

After you travel a short distance and feel the horse is relaxing, let it spread its wings a bit. Move it to one side or the other of the horse in front and urge it to walk a bit faster so that it is now beside the horse that was in front. Your companion will still be in the lead, so the young horse is learning to step out a bit on its own, but still can draw confidence from the horse your companion is riding.

Eventually, you will want to move up so that you are riding beside your companion and, ultimately, let the young horse take the lead. Don't overdo it that first ride. A couple of

Leading a young horse on the first trail ride.

miles is plenty. Remember, the youngster is still learning to carry your weight and maintain proper balance. This will cause it to tire quickly and you do want to end this first ride on a positive note, with the young horse still fresh and looking for more new adventures.

You should know the trail well for that first ride. This is not the time to encounter fallen trees or mud holes. They should come a bit later after the horse has gained more confidence. The first rides should be enjoyable, but not challenging to the young horse. After a ride or two, have your companion move out at a trot and then a lope or canter with the young horse following behind. Make certain that the trail is free of obstacles when you do this the first time.

After a few pleasant, easy rides, you can think about challenging the young horse a bit more. One of the greatest challenges for most young horses is wet ground. There is a reason for this. It is an inherited fear that you as the handler and number one individual in the young horse's life must understand and know how to handle.

We have already mentioned that the horse has always been a prey animal. Its greatest weapon against predators was, and still is, flight. Wild horses know instinctively that if they become mired in a muddy spot, they are easy pickings for predators of the cat family that can walk across a surface on wide paws that will not bear the weight of a horse with its sharp hooves. Therefore, wild horses for centuries avoided such traps and that inherent fear has been passed down and still exists in horses that have never lived a day in the wild.

The only way you can overcome this inherent fear is to

demonstrate to the horse that you will not ask it to go anywhere that is unsafe. This means that you must pick the spot for that first water-crossing lesson with caution. The best place is a stream with a hard, pebbly bottom that is no deeper than the horse's knees and is too wide for the youngster to jump.

It is important that the spot you pick is one where going through the water is the only option available if the horse is to continue moving forward. It makes no sense to attempt to force a horse through a water puddle when there is dry ground on both sides. In that scenario, one will be asking the horse to do something that it would never do on its own. If there is a way around a wet spot, its instincts tell it to take that route.

For this lesson, you again need the help of another rider on a calm horse. Ride up to the water and let your young horse look and sniff. Sometimes, especially if the horse was born and raised in open country where it had to cross wet areas, the lesson will be short and sweet with the young horse readily entering the water.

Expect that to be the exception rather than the rule. Most young horses will be very apprehensive about entering a river or crossing a wet area the first time. Ask your companion to ride into the water and across to the other side. The young horse now can see that its equine companion is unafraid. As the other horse enters the water, urge the youngster to follow. If it resists, have your companion return to your side, turn and ride into the water again, this time stopping midway across. Again, urge the young horse to follow.

Normally, the youngster will draw confidence from the other horse and enter the water. It may become frightened and rush across that first time. Don't try to stop it. Let it cross in a hurry, but as soon as you reach the other side, turn it about and ask it to cross to the opposite bank. The crossing and re-crossing should continue until the young horse walks quietly through the water and even stops in midstream when so cued.

If the young horse is overly resistant, you might want to dismount and use a halter and lead shank as aids. You are the one doing the teaching, so borrow your companion's horse. With lead shank in hand, ride the other horse into the water and stop, using pressure on the halter to get the young horse to follow. This is where the early leading building blocks will pay off. The horse has it ingrained in its mind that it must yield to pressure and in most cases will do so, aided by the confidence it has in the horse that is already standing in the water.

Crossing water for the first time behind a trusted older horse.

It is a good idea to take a lunge whip to the crossing spot as well as halter and lead shank. If the horse still refuses, your companion on the ground can add further pressure with light flicks of the lunge whip against the young horse's hocks.

This is not a time to be impatient. The important thing is that the session does not end until the horse crosses the water. Do not start such a session unless you know you have the time and patience to see it to a proper conclusion.

The beauty of trail riding is that you can teach the horse many things it doesn't realize it is being taught. Responding quickly and easily to light rein pressure is a case in point. If you are an English rider, you will be using the direct rein and the indirect rein. The direct rein is used to effect a change in direction and is a tug somewhat outward and to the rear. The indirect rein is used to help position the horse's body. It is applied with rein pressure both against the horse's neck and rearward on the bit.

In western riding, you will want the horse to respond to neck reining. With neck reining you merely lay the rein against the horse's neck and that cues it to move in the opposite direction.

Your goal should be to attain immediate response from the horse with the lightest of pressure. You can work on this while trail riding by directing the horse toward an obstacle that it can't pass over, but must go to one side or the other. Decide in advance to which side the horse should go, and just when the horse realizes it is decision time, apply pressure for a turn in the direction you have chosen. The horse will realize that it had to turn one way or the other to get around the object, so its response to rein pressure was a natural thing to do.

It's not so scary after all.

While working on these training building blocks, you can and should use your body as an aid.

When teaching neck reining, for example, you can give the horse multiple signals in telling it which direction it should turn. When you come to an object and decide to pass it on the left, provide a bit of pressure via direct rein with your left hand. Simultaneously lay the right rein against the horse's neck and shift your body weight a bit to the left and press the calf of your right leg against the horse's side at the girth or cinch. Don't lean, just put more weight in the left stirrup and apply pressure with your right leg. With repetition, the horse will soon learn to turn with only a slight shifting of your weight and as time goes, you can guide it with leg pressure only.

During these early sessions, you also can work on achieving a prompt halt with only minimal pressure on the bit. Again, the body is used as an aid. Start by combining voice command, light pressure on the bit, and a sinking of your weight into the saddle. Work your way to the point where you can quickly bring the horse to a stop with a voice command only, or with an almost imperceptible raising of the rein hand, combined with sinking your weight into the saddle.

A vice that can crop up in the young horse at this stage of its training is the refusal to stand while you mount and dismount. This is a vice that is easier to prevent than to cure. When riding the young horse during those early sessions — and later as

Standing quietly as the rider mounts.

well — always make it stand for a few moments after you mount. If you jump aboard and head right off at a trot, the horse soon will equate mounting with instant forward motion and before long will be moving out before you have a foot in the stirrup. If this training building block is put firmly in place when the horse is first mounted and ridden, it will never know there is another option.

It is the same with dismounting. Don't pop down from the horse while it is still on the move. Bring it to a halt and wait until it is standing quietly before you dismount. In both mounting and dismounting, you will find the voice command to "Whoa" or "Hup" to be helpful if the horse is inclined to move.

Solving the problem if you have purchased a horse with the vice requires time and patience. With the reins in your left hand, put your foot in the stirrup and pause. If the horse attempts to move, immediately check it by applying pressure on the bit. Don't make an attempt to mount until the horse is standing still. When it is standing, put weight in the stirrup, but be prepared to step back down quickly and once again check the horse if it attempts to move.

The important thing is that you do not swing all the way into the saddle until the horse is standing quietly. Once aboard, do not let the horse move off. Instead, ask it to stand, then dismount and do the whole thing over again.

AVOID FRIGHTENING SITUATIONS

The young horse shouldn't be taken for rides along busy roads or highways unless some desensitizing has been done at home first. Make sure that it is used to cars, trucks, tractors, motorcycles, or other vehicles before challenging it with a ride along a road. This should be done in the safety and security of the yard at home. Ask someone to drive a vehicle around the horse while you are riding. Do the same with a bicycle and motorcycle, if possible. Bikes and motorcycles frighten most horses when they first come into contact with them. It is perhaps because they have difficulty focusing on a narrow object that is moving rapidly.

Getting used to strange objects.

You also can expect the young horse to be frightened of objects that are waving in the air. There is a reason for this and the handler or rider should understand it. The horse, as mentioned, has monocular and binocular vision. Though its range of vision is extremely broad, it isn't acute unless the horse has an opportunity to stop and focus its eyes. At the same time, the horse has hearing that is far more acute than ours.

Thus, if you are riding down a forested trail during high

wind, the horse will be desperately trying to focus on a variety of moving branches and leaves that won't hold still and its ears will be assaulted by a barrage of sound. The combination can result in a horse that becomes extremely agitated. The rider can't help the horse focus its eyes nor relieve the cacophony of sound. What the rider can do is be very calm and reassuring, using a quiet voice to help steady the jittery horse.

Negotiating a small obstacle.

The horse also has a very large retina and when it looks at objects, they appear larger than they would to a human. The neighbor's dog that comes bounding out, for example, will appear to be just that to you, but to the horse, it might appear to be the size of a Shetland pony. Again, the role of the rider is to remain calm and confident, transmitting those emotions to the horse.

Many of the building blocks discussed above also can be developed in a corral or arena. If you lack trails, but have access to an arena, add some aids. Place a barrel in the middle of the arena, for example, to help teach response to reining cues. Put poles on the ground, so that the horse learns to negotiate its way without striking them. Put up a small jump, so the horse learns to hop over an obstacle that is too high to be stepped over.

You also can use the walls or fences of the arena to your advantage. Ride the horse directly at a fence, then cue it to turn either left or right. Riding toward the fence also can be effective when cueing for the halt. The horse realizes that it can't go through the fence, so it must turn one way or the other or come to a stop.

If you merely ride the horse in circles in the arena, it will soon become bored. Variety is one of the greatest aids in teaching the young horse. Once we have reached a point where horse and rider are confident in each other, it might be time to head off somewhere else for a trail ride or a different arena.

CHAPTER 9

Trailer Loading

Few things are more traumatic for the average horse owner than a horse which refuses to load into a trailer. In addition to being frustrating and time-consuming, the non-loader also can cause injury to itself as well as to the humans attempting to load it.

There is always a reason why a horse doesn't want to enter a trailer. One reason that crops up repeatedly is very basic. The horse doesn't want to be confined. Other reasons might include bad experiences because of erratic or improper driving of the vehicle towing the trailer. Whatever the reason, refusal to enter the trailer is a problem that must be solved or much of your previous training will be for naught. The young horse might be well trained in all other aspects, but if you can't get it off the place other than by riding, its usefulness is compromised.

Before training or retraining a horse to load into a trailer, we must understand the problems that are causing the refusal. As mentioned, many horses do not

Horses don't like to be confined.

like being confined. The horse is claustrophobic by nature, and for good reason. We need only look to horses in the wild to understand this fear. Wild horses always will avoid being trapped in an area where there is not at least one clear avenue of escape. Nature gave them the gift of flight to escape predators and, when left to their own devices in the wild, they almost always will keep themselves in a position to flee.

This means that they do not allow themselves to be trapped in confining box canyons, even though taking refuge there might protect them from wind and rain. Instead, they will find a spot next to a high bluff or bank that will break the wind. Though the protection is only one-sided, they are left with three open escape routes.

By domesticating the horse, we have somewhat alleviated this fear of being imprisoned, but we have not obliterated it. By asking a horse to enter a strange, enclosed area, such as a trailer, we help rekindle this inherent fear.

By realizing that the horse is claustrophobic by nature, you can approach trailer loading in a manner that is both sympathetic and firm. Your sympathy is in response to the knowledge that the horse is acting out of fear. But you also must be firm, or the horse's fear will be exacerbated with every successful refusal.

As with most everything else involved with training horses, there are about as many approaches to solving the problem as there are people faced with the dilemma. There are some who believe that the appropriate way is to use a rope behind the horse's rear end and force it into the trailer. The problem with this approach, when it is successful, is that you are pretty much stuck with using that rope forever. Many horses

> ## AT A GLANCE
>
> - Bad experiences can cause a horse to refuse to load.
>
> - If a mare is an easy loader, her foal can be taught quickly how to load.
>
> - Patience is needed for loading problem horses and first-timers.
>
> - Never tie a horse in a trailer until the rear door is closed and never open a rear door until the horse is untied.

so trained will stand at the trailer entrance until they feel pressure from the rope.

Still other folks approach the problem in a passive way. They will haul the trailer into the center of a corral and place the horse's feed and water inside. When the horse is hungry or thirsty enough, it is theorized, it will enter the trailer to obtain food and water. This approach can be successful, but the horse is learning to enter the trailer only when it is hungry or thirsty.

Then there are those who simply use brute force. The horse is physically pulled or pushed into the trailer and the door slammed behind it. This is the worst possible approach.

There is a better way than those listed above. It combines kindness and firmness. We are faced with something of a Catch-22 situation when trying to load a frightened horse. We want to overcome its fear of getting into the trailer, but the only way we can accomplish that is by first getting it into the trailer.

Before discussing the "better" approach in detail, it should be pointed out that trailer loading problems can be avoided if the foal is taught to enter the trailer at a very early age. The best-case scenario is for the dam of the foal to be an easy loader. When that is the situation, you can turn the foal into an easy loader in short order.

Use either a stock trailer or a trailer where the stall partitions have been removed. This approach is a two-person job. One person leads the mare into the trailer while also having in hand a lead shank attached to the foal's halter. The second person stands by to give the foal a boost if it doesn't follow. At this stage of its life, the foal still depends on its mother for security. If she readily enters the trailer, it is a good bet that the foal will hop right in behind her. If it doesn't, a gentle boost by the helper will get the job done.

Once the dam and foal are in the trailer, let them stand there for a few minutes and then back them out. Repeat that process a couple of times each day for several days and the foal should never become a loading or unloading problem. After several loading sessions, take the two of them for a short, but easy ride.

To make loading and unloading of the foal a more pleasant experience, you should try to eliminate the need for the youngster to take a big step up into the trailer. This means that you should back the trailer into a depression or ditch so that the step up and down is only a small one.

If the foal's dam is a problem loader, the above approach would be totally inappropriate. The foal would instantly feed off the mother's fear and also would refuse to enter the trailer. When that is the case, the first loading session should be put off until after the youngster is weaned.

The toughest horses to load are those that once entered a trailer willingly only to be traumatized by an erratic and thoughtless driver who took corners too fast and started and stopped abruptly. These are horses whose worst fears have been realized and, in the process, have become dead set against ever re-entering a trailer. They can be taught to enter a trailer again, but it will take a number of trips without trauma before they will overcome their deep-seated fears.

The approach for loading problem horses and first timers involves a good deal of patience. We already have discussed at length that training horses, to a large extent, involves getting them to move away from pressure. When loading, that pressure will be applied both with intermittent tugs on the lead shank and from the rear with taps from a lunge whip. You also can use a stiff fishing rod with a piece of plastic on the end or even a broom in lieu of the lunge whip. I favor the lunge whip because its length provides a built-in safety factor for the person using it.

This approach requires either a stock trailer or one with the stall partitions removed. The trailer also should be parked, as much as possible, in an area where the horse does not have to negotiate a high step upward. The trailer also should be parked against a solid wall to close off one escape route.

It also is good to have a limited amount of space behind the trailer. You do not want the horse to be tightly boxed in, but you do not want unlimited freedom to the rear.

A third avenue of escape for the horse will be cut off by the person who is assisting. Thus, the only real viable place for the horse to go in response to pressure is into the trailer. Proper timing in applying pressure is a key element. Equally important are copious quantities of time and patience. Teaching a first timer or problem loader to enter and depart a trailer should not be started unless you are prepared to see it through to a satisfactory conclusion, even though it might take a couple of hours. Above all, there is no room for anger on the part of the people involved. You must remember that the horse is refusing to enter the trailer because of fear. It isn't trying to thwart and frustrate you.

Before a session gets under way, the two people loading must understand their individual roles and be able to communicate without articulating a lot of instructions. Three pieces of equipment are required: a lead shank snapped into the halter ring, a lunge whip, and a lunge line with chain and snap at one end. The lunge line is something of a court of last resort.

Begin the process by establishing a friendly relationship with the horse. Lead it about. Pet it and praise it in a low, steady voice. When the horse is relaxed, lead it to the rear of the trailer. If it doesn't want to approach the trailer right away, don't force the issue. Alleviate its fears with more low-voiced talking and a lot of petting and scratching.

When you feel the horse relax, apply pressure on the lead shank, asking it to move forward. Keep inching your way along until the horse is right up to the trailer. At this point, step into the trailer and urge the horse to follow with tugs on the lead shank. Your helper is a quiet bystander.

Please bear in mind that any time you step into a confined area and ask a horse to step in with you, there is an element of danger involved. It is for this reason that you should be working with an open stock trailer or one with the partitions removed. Never, never ask a horse to follow you into the single stall of a trailer. The moment the horse enters, you are trapped. An escape door can provide a measure of protection, but the horse just might follow you right through it and become injured.

Once the horse relaxes in the trailer, repeat the loading process.

If the horse doesn't instantly follow you into the trailer, be patient. Pet it, scratch it, and keep up your low monotone vocal encouragement. Then, step back further into the trailer and apply pressure with another tug on the lead shank.

If the horse puts one foot into the trailer and then pulls back, immediately relax the pressure. To keep tugging at this point will stimulate the trapped feeling. However, it is important that the horse continue to face the trailer's open door. Throughout this entire process, the horse must stay focused on the trailer and not be allowed to wander away from it.

Keep working with the horse in this manner until you sense that it has gone as far as it is going to with only this form of pressure. When that is the case, ask your helper to tap the horse on the hocks gently with the lunge whip. We are not talking about slashes with the whip here, just gentle taps to provide a form of pressure from the rear.

Often, this is all the extra encouragement required, and the horse will step inside the trailer. When it is inside, do not close the door behind it. Let it stand there and adjust to its new surroundings, knowing that the escape door to the rear is still open. If it wants to back out, let it. But then, immediately ask it to enter the trailer again. Once the horse has relaxed, back it out or turn it about and lead it out and then reload.

If you are dealing with a problem loader, do not move the trailer after the first several loadings. Just load and unload the horse until you sense that it is relaxing and overcoming its fear. When you do drive off, make it the most careful ride the horse has ever experienced — slow starts, gentle stops, and no curves at speed.

While the above approach will get most horses loaded, there is always a minority that will carry determination to stay out of the trailer a step further. These are horses that will run backward away from the trailer. Having a solid wall or fence to the rear will limit that escape route. The helper with the lunge whip will eliminate it further. When the horse repeatedly runs backward, the helper should use the lash of the lunge whip to give it a serious crack around the hocks.

The moment the horse comes to a stop, pressure should be applied with tugs on the lead shank and gentle taps on the hocks. The sharp crack of the whip is used only when the horse is repeatedly backing away from the trailer at speed. If the horse persists in evading the trailer, it is time for the final piece of equipment — the lunge line with chain at the end. Run the chain through the left outside halter ring, over the horse's nose, through the right side ring, then fasten it to the high ring on the right side of the halter.

You are now using two lines — one in each hand. One is the lead shank and the other is the lunge line. The lead shank continues to provide pressure for forward movement. The lunge line is used only when the horse moves backward at speed. When the horse backs away, apply pressure with the lunge line. The chain over the nose will create discomfort. It is unnecessary to do a lot of jerking on the lunge line. Merely hold to it firmly while moving forward as the horse moves rearward. Couple this pressure with your helper administering a sharp crack around the hocks with the lunge whip. The moment the horse comes to halt, relax the pressure on the lunge line and quietly apply pressure to go forward with the lead shank. Simultaneously, your helper should be tapping the horse lightly on the hocks with the lunge whip.

The moment the horse takes a step forward, relax all forms of pressure. If it takes a few steps and stops, let it relax for a few moments. Pett and talk quietly to the horse. Then, resume the pressure to move forward with tugs on the lunge line and taps from the whip. Before long the trailer will appear to be a haven for the horse. While it is outside and evading the trailer, it is finding life quite uncomfortable. Eventually, it will take refuge in the trailer. The moment the horse appears ready to step inside, all pressure should cease so it has an opportunity to enter on its own. Once the horse is inside, pet it, praise it, then allow it to exit. Load and unload several times during that first session. Repeat the process the next day and the day after until the horse willingly enters the trailer with little or no pressure being applied.

Two rules of thumb to remember when loading and unloading horses: Never tie a horse inside the trailer until the rear door is closed, and never open a rear door until the horse is untied.

The next step in the learning process involves teaching the horse to enter a single stall of a trailer. You can use a version of the approach described above, with one key difference. Never ask the horse to enter the stall you are occupying. Instead, enter that stall and close the bottom half of the door. Then, with the lead line running through the opposite door which is open, apply pressure with tugs to ask the horse to enter the other stall. If you have been diligent in teaching it to enter the open trailer, this step should be easy.

Once the horse is entering the single stall in that manner, it is time for the final training step. With only one door of the trailer open, lead the horse forward and ask it to enter the trailer on its own. Have your helper standing by to gently encourage it with light taps on the hocks.

Your ultimate goal is a horse that walks right into the trailer with no pressure applied and with no one inside the trailer with it.

CHAPTER 10
Proper Equipment

When training the young horse we sometimes are faced with problems that stem from ill-fitting equipment. A bit that doesn't fit properly could result in a horse tossing its head in irritation. An improperly fitted saddle might make the horse sore backed, to the point where being ridden is a painful experience. A one-eared bridle might fit so tightly that it is a constant source of irritation to a very sensitive part of the horse's anatomy. The list goes on.

Before you can understand what constitutes an ill-fitting piece of equipment, you must recognize what is involved in a proper fit.

BITS

We begin with bits. This is a subject that could command hours of discussion and the writing of hundreds of thousands of words. I choose to simplify it because for the young horse in training, there is one basic bit that should be used: the snaffle.

Of course, even the basic snaffle comes in a variety of sizes, shapes, and designs. I prefer either the D-ring or the loose-ring snaffle with a jointed mouthpiece that is of moderate size. A mouthpiece that is very narrow can put painful pressure on the corners of the horse's mouth. One that is overly large might be uncomfortable and not produce appropriate pressure to elicit the desired response.

The training goal, as far as bits are concerned, should be to get maximum response with minimum pressure. In the beginning, however, this will seem difficult. Often, when we give just a tiny little tug on the reins, the horse continues on its way without seeming to notice. It is for this reason that you must concentrate on using legs and body language to help in the communications department.

AT A GLANCE

• The snaffle is the one basic bit that should be used in training a young horse.

• A horse with a properly fitted bit will respond to rein pressure without opening its mouth.

• A well-fitted saddle allows a horse to carry a rider for hours without suffering pain.

Also, in the beginning, the signals are exaggerated. Instead of a gentle tug, you often must reach out with a hand and give a firm pull in the direction you want the horse to turn. Then, as the horse begins to get the message, lighter and lighter tugs are used until only a touch is needed.

Because you must use some firmness in the beginning, it is imperative that the bit be properly fitted to the horse's mouth and the mouthpiece not be so small in circumference that it makes the corners of the mouth sore.

After deciding on the cheekpieces — D-ring, loose-ring, or whatever — and the size of the mouthpiece, there is a highly important third element to be considered — width of the mouth piece. The distance between the cheekpieces should be the same distance as the width of the horse's mouth; no more, no less. It is not a case of one size fits all.

A petite Arabian, for example, might require a mouthpiece that is four and one-half to four and three-quarters inches in width while a big warmblood may require one that is five inches wide or more. The proper fit will be a bit where the cheekpieces rest lightly against each side of the muzzle area when not in use. If the bit is too large, it will slide back and forth in irritating fashion each time a direct rein is applied in

D-ring snaffle.

one direction or the other. If the bit is too small, the pinching effect will be a source of constant irritation and distraction to the horse.

Once the correct size has been determined, the next important step is to hang it properly in the young horse's mouth. When the bridle is in place, the bit should be resting comfortably against the corners of the mouth on each side. If the bit is causing the horse to "smile" with one or two wrinkles at the corners, the bit is too tight. If it is hanging below the corners, it is too loose.

Sometimes, it is necessary to punch new holes in the bridle to obtain a comfortable fit.

A horse that is carrying a properly fitted bit will be one that works the mouthpiece gently with its tongue and will respond readily to rein pressure without opening its mouth. As mentioned earlier, I favor a snaffle with rollers to encourage the horse to work its tongue back and forth, causing it to salivate and thus providing itself with natural lubrication at the corners of the mouth.

Care also should be taken in fitting the bridle to the horse's head. Some horses have narrow, short heads while others are long and broad. Again, one size does not fit all. A one-eared bridle that has a small opening for the ear can be a source of constant irritation and discomfort to a horse with large ears.

The same is true of bridles with browbands. If the browband is too narrow, it can be a painful irritant. The throat latch should be long enough to rest lightly against the throat, but should not be so tight that it hinders the breathing process.

The weight of the reins can have a bearing on the horse's ability to learn neck reining in western riding. I prefer heavy reins that the horse can feel when one or the other is pressed against its neck. When riding the young horse in English tack, I prefer broad, braided reins that are easily gripped, and are relatively lightweight.

With some horses, such as racing Thoroughbreds, the

snaffle bit, or some variation of it, might be all that the horse carries throughout its career. With others, there will be more sophisticated mouthwear, ranging from the shanked curb for western riding to a combination of curb and light snaffle for English-type show horses.

A variety of snaffle bits.

When a horse is going from the snaffle to another bit, I think the transition should be as gradual as possible. With horses that are heading for a career in some form of western riding, I prefer a light curb bit with only a slight curvature to the port or mouthpiece. This transition bit should have shanks that can rotate against the side of the mouthpiece, making it easier to direct rein the young horse.

It is also important that the transition bit, and all others for that matter, be properly balanced. You can check this by picking up the bridle by the headstall. As you look down at the bit, it should have a slight rearward tilt. This will enable the bit to lay gently against the horse's tongue and not be in contact with other parts of the inner mouth when the reins are slack.

With the horse that is heading toward English pursuits, an appropriate transition bit is the single mouthpiece pelham that has attachment for four reins.

More sophisticated bits might be in the offing as the horse develops, but by then it will have passed out of the basic training stages that are being discussed here.

When switching to a transition bit, the chin strap or chain must fit properly. Just how this should be fitted will vary from horse to horse, but the rule of thumb is that you should be able to insert two fingers between the chin strap or chain and the horse's jaw. When that is the case, you can take up the reins and apply light pressure without making instant use of the leverage that the shanks of the bit, combined with curb strap or chain, make possible.

A twisted chin chain should never be used on the young horse in training because it is far too severe. The chin chain should be of the heavier, rolled variety, whether riding English or western.

When making the transition from snaffle to a form of curb, you should be soft and gentle with the hands, especially during those first few rides. Remember that you are using a different form of pressure on the horse's mouth. With the snaffle, almost all of the pressure was on the corners of the mouth. Now you are engaging the tongue, the bars of the horse's mouth, and the sensitive area of the chin.

Before making the transition, the horse should be responsive to leg cues and shifts of body weight so that only minimal pressure is applied to the reins when turning or stopping.

A word about bit maintenance. How you handle a bit after riding has much to do with its longevity and comfort to the horse. It is a good practice to wipe the bit dry each time after removing it from the horse's mouth to make certain that moisture is removed, along with bits of hay or grass that can dry and harden on the surface and cause discomfort the next time it is placed in the horse's mouth.

You also should examine the bit very closely on a frequent basis. Some horses chew on the bit and in the course of time, create ridges or sharp projections that can cause pain and irritation to the mouth. A bit that has become rusty as the result of weeks of non-use without proper care also can be a source of mouth irritation.

SADDLES

A properly fitted saddle will allow the horse to carry a rider long hours without suffering pain. An ill-fitting saddle causes irritation from the moment it is placed on the horse's back until it is removed. Unfortunately, it is a more difficult proposition to have that perfectly fitted saddle than the perfectly fitted bridle and bit. As with bits, one size does not fit all.

If the same saddle is used on an angular Thoroughbred with high, sharp withers as is used on the broad back of a chunky Quarter Horse, for example, there are going to be comfort problems for one or the other.

Another problem with saddle fit involves the various stages through which a horse goes during a riding season. At the beginning of the season, the horse's body might be quite wide after a few months lay-up. As the horse begins rounding into shape, the body will become narrower as muscles harden. If it is involved in a long, hard season of eventing or other athletic endeavor, the body will become even narrower. Thus, a saddle that fit this horse properly in the spring, might not fit it properly in the fall.

Still another problem involves economics. Saddles are expensive and having a different one for each phase of the horse's conditioning program is prohibitive for most owners.

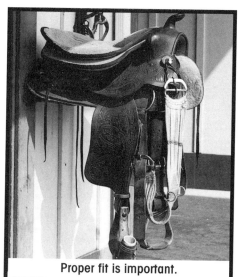

Proper fit is important.

It is a must that the saddle fit properly once the horse has rounded into good physical condition and is being used regularly. It is also highly important that the horse be monitored on a ride-by-ride basis for back soreness. If the back does become sore because of the saddle, the owner has no recourse but to find a saddle that fits or the horse soon will be unrideable. When the horse is suffering from a sore back because of an ill-fitting saddle, the results can be either mild or disastrous — ranging from a casual protest when being saddled to full-fledged bucking that puts the rider's life and limb at risk.

Be aware that pain can be inflicted to a horse's back even though the saddle fits properly. I am referring to pain that is rider-induced as the result of improper position and poor balance.

The first step in checking for back pain in the young training horse is to palpate firmly with the fingers along the middle of the muscles running down either side of the spine. (They are called the longissimus dorsi muscles.) If the horse is in pain, it will react by contracting its back muscles. It is important to learn what is a normal contraction as the result of palpating pressure and what is elicited as the result of pain. This means that before you begin riding the horse, the back should be palpated so that there is a base for comparison.

There are some other obvious signs when a saddle is not properly fitted, including obvious sores, white hairs under the saddle, temporary swelling after the saddle is removed, scars or hard spots in the muscle or skin, and atrophy of the muscles on the sides of the withers. If any of the these signs show up during palpation and observation, it is time to do a serious check on saddle fit and riding balance.

If the gullet — the open area of the pommel — is too wide, the saddle will bring weight to bear on the horse's withers, causing soreness to a part of the anatomy that is not designed to carry weight. If the gullet is too narrow, the saddle will sit up too high and weight will be improperly distributed.

Weight should be evenly distributed over the panels or underside of the saddle. The panels must be wide enough to offer good support without losing the contour needed to fit the horse's back. The gullet should be wide enough to allow the spine complete freedom from pressure and to allow the spine to bend slightly during movement.

A properly fitted saddle will be level when viewed from the side. There is a double problem when saddles aren't level.

First, they will be uncomfortable to the horse. Second, the rider will not be able to sit properly and this will cause additional discomfort and pain to the horse.

When viewed from the side, a saddle that is too narrow at the withers generally will be high at the pommel while a saddle that is too wide at the withers will be high at the cantle.

It should be noted that the way in which a saddle is placed on a horse's back also influences how level it will be. Perhaps the most frequently encountered positioning problem involves placing the saddle too far forward on the horse's back. This means that the rigid tree is over the scapula. Putting the saddle in this position serves to restrict the movement of the front legs and will irritate the horse each and every step.

There is a "sweet spot" on every horse's back where the saddle, if properly fitted, is carried comfortably. When training the young horse, you must find this spot and position the saddle properly each time the horse is ridden. If it can't be found, it might mean that a different saddle is needed.

CHAPTER 11
Health and Nutritional Needs

When training the young horse, you must be conscious of some special health and nutritional needs. One of the primary health concerns, especially during hot summer weather, involves prevention of overheating during training and proper cooling out after a training session. Problems also can arise when training in cold weather. Let's first take a look at cooling the horse following hot weather training sessions.

The only mammal, other than man, which cools itself primarily by sweating is the horse. There is some heat dissipation via other routes, such as respiration, but very little. The horse must sweat in order to cool itself. Of course, there is a little more to it than just simply saying a horse must sweat.

First of all, there must be ample blood flow to carry heat from the core of the horse's body to the blood vessels near the skin. The problem is that when blood is needed to carry heat to the skin, it also is needed by working muscles and other tissues throughout the body. This means that the heart must work much harder.

As heat increases within the horse's body, it becomes increasingly difficult for the animal to maintain proper blood volume and flow. As the heart pumps harder and harder to increase blood flow so that the horse can fuel muscle action and dissipate heat through sweating, progressive dehydration and loss of plasma water from the bloodstream occur. This, in turn, results in a decrease in circulating blood volume. At this point, the horse's heart is called on for an even greater effort. It must increase the cardiac output by beating faster.

When dehydration reaches the point at which even a more rapidly beating heart can't compensate, body temperature continues to rise and the horse suffers from fatigue and an inability to perform at its previous level. Unless steps are taken to lower body temperature, the horse eventually won't be able to perform at all and its life may be at risk.

> ## AT A GLANCE
>
> • Other than man, the horse is the only mammal which cools itself mainly by sweating.
>
> • Water is the best way to combat overheating.
>
> • During cold weather, properly cooling out a horse can be a challenge.
>
> • Feed a horse by weight, not by measure.

If a horse's body temperature soars to 105 or 106 degrees Fahrenheit without proper cooling being administered, heat stroke and other thermal injuries can result.

The best weapon in the world to combat overheating and to help in the cooling down process is water — taken both internally and applied externally.

There is no magic formula as to how much water a horse should consume at rest or during and after exercise. It will vary from horse to horse. The National Research Council, which has established a set of guidelines for equine food and water consumption, recommends that a horse consume 2 to 4 liters of water per kilogram of feed intake. A liter corresponds to 1.057 quarts of liquid and a kilogram corresponds to 2.2046 pounds.

However, you should bear in mind that the above is only a very general recommendation. It doesn't take into account wide variances in temperature. A horse will drink much more when the weather is hot than when cool temperatures prevail.

A horse's water requirement can jump 15% to 20% during

hot weather. If the horse is involved in heavy exercise during the heat of the day, the water needs and/or consumption can increase by as much as 300%. This means that under certain heat and exercise conditions a horse might consume as much as 25 gallons of water.

That might sound like a great deal of water, but it really isn't when you consider that the horse can lose up to four gallons of liquid per hour through sweating. It quickly becomes obvious that the exercising horse must replace the liquids it is losing or dehydration will result.

Heavy sweating by the young horse in training also depletes and disrupts the horse's supply and balance of electrolytes. These are the salts and minerals that play a key role in keeping the equine body functioning properly. Under normal circumstances, the horse will maintain a balanced supply of electrolytes through an appropriate diet and by having access to salt and minerals. However, when the horse exercises heavily during hot weather, the electrolyte loss will be so rapid and so great that its body soon comes up short and electrolytes must be supplemented via the water the horse is consuming.

Time to learn a new term. It is hypertonic. A horse's sweat is termed as being hypertonic. This means that it contains a significant amount of two key electrolytes: sodium or salt and potassium. When profuse sweating lowers the level of these two electrolytes, along with others, the horse may suffer fatigue and muscle cramps.

If you are working a young horse in the early stages of training under severely hot conditions, the danger of electrolyte loss — especially salt and potassium — is greater than it would be for a well-conditioned horse. The reason is that when the horse rounds into good physical condition, its body sets into motion certain mechanisms designed to conserve sodium when the animal is sweating. There will be far less salt in the sweat of a conditioned horse than in the sweat of one that is not in good physical condition.

When training in hot weather, it is a good idea to provide some electrolyte supplementation if it sweats profusely. Packages of electrolytes in powder form are available commercially and can be dissolved in the horse's water.

Of course, if the horse refuses to drink, water will not be consumed and the electrolytes will not be ingested. Some horses drink copious quantities of water while others will only sip. The key thing, especially for the

Offer a horse water several times during a training session.

sippers, is to offer the young horse water several times during a training session in hot weather, rather than wait until the session is over.

There is another negative factor that often is associated with heat — humidity. As already mentioned, the horse's prime method for cooling is to sweat and for the sweat to evaporate from the skin. When humidity is high, there is very little evaporation and the cooling down process is compromised. When humidity is very high, the horse's body heat is actually trapped by the sweat that doesn't evaporate, rather than being liberated.

Equine researchers have done a great deal of study on the effects of heat and humidity. They have found what has been termed a comfort zone for horses. Understanding what constitutes this comfort zone will provide the trainer with a healthy guideline of activity for the young horse in training.

To compute the comfort zone, add the temperature of the day in degrees Fahrenheit with that day's percentage figure for humidity. If the total is below 130, the horse is operating within an easy comfort zone. When the total is between 130 and 150, horses will sweat when exercised, but there should be no heat and humidity-related problems if the animal drinks an adequate amount of water.

Trouble begins rearing its head when the index or total reaches 150 and the humidity is higher than 75%. At that total, the horse's comfort zone is gone because heat dissipation becomes a problem even if the horse drinks a lot of water.

Serious trouble can be in store for the heavily exercising horse when the index exceeds 180. At this level, the normal routes of heat dissipation in a horse's body don't work well at all and strenuous exercise should be avoided.

With the above knowledge as background, you can plan a training program and cooling out procedure that will prevent thermal injury to the horse.

When the days are hot and humid, training sessions should be planned for early in the cool morning hours or later in the afternoon or evening after the heat of the day breaks. If the horse must be trained during the hottest part of the day, the session should be brief and not too strenuous.

During the session and after it is over, the horse should be allowed to drink all of the water it desires. But if the horse is very thirsty and the water very cold, allow the horse to drink only a gallon or two, then walk it a bit, and offer a similar amount of water. By repeating this approach until the horse has satisfied its thirst, it can consume an adequate amount of water in a short span of time without danger.

Washing down a horse during hot weather.

The best way to facilitate the cooling process is by washing down the horse with either a hose or sponge. Be prepared for the young horse to become frightened the first time you turn the hose on it. Start by having only a trickle coming out of the hose, rather than a full stream under pressure. Very quickly, the young horse will recognize that the hose means relief from heat and will relish it.

One of the most important pieces of equipment at this juncture is a scraper for removing excess water from the horse's coat. You want moisture that will evaporate and cool. What you

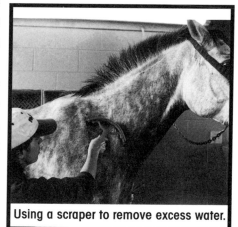
Using a scraper to remove excess water.

don't want is a lot of water remaining on the horse's body. It will very quickly become warm and trap the horse's heat, the same thing that happens on a hot and humid day.

Close observation is a good ally. You must learn how much heat stresses the young horse and what is required to cool it out quickly.

When training a horse during cold weather, we are faced with a different set of concerns. Overheating is rarely a problem, but getting a horse properly cooled out can be challenging. The prime reason is that the horse's hair is long and heavy during the cold weather months and can act as insulation.

The hair is good insulation only when it is dry and fluffed up. In that condition, it can shield the skin from wind and insulate it against cold. When the hair is wet from sweat and plastered against the skin, it can neither shield nor insulate.

While water is a staunch ally in the cooling out process during hot weather, our chief ally in cold weather is the blanket. Without the help of blankets in cold weather, the horse might cool out too quickly and be in danger of catching a cold or even pneumonia. This is especially true if the wind is blowing.

This does not mean that we should pile heavy blankets on the sweating horse. If the covering is too heavy and too well-insulated, it might trap the moisture between the skin and blanket, preventing the hair from returning to its dry, fluffy state.

A better approach is to cover the young horse with a light blanket after a training session, then lead it about until the hair is at least semi-dry. The exercise from walking keeps the body from cooling too rapidly and the light blanket protects from the wind and cold air while still allowing the moisture to evaporate and the hair to dry.

When the horse's coat is dry, it is time to remove what is by now a damp light blanket. Depending on wind and weather conditions, you might either allow the horse to be unblanketed or, if there is a cold wind, to be covered with what can now be a heavy blanket.

NUTRITIONAL NEEDS

When we take a young horse from a life of leisure and begin training it, we must also understand that there will be a change in the animal's nutritional needs. Because it is burning up more energy, the young horse in training will need more "fuel" for its tank.

It is important that you feed the horse by weight, not by measure. The traditional measuring device for grain is the three-pound coffee can. We must be aware that a three-pound coffee can filled with oats will weigh less than the same can filled with corn. When filled with light oats, the can might weigh only 2 or 2½ pounds. The same can filled with corn might weigh 5 pounds.

It is the same with hay. A large fluffy flake of grass hay might weigh far less than a smaller flake of firmly packed alfalfa.

Grain should be added to the diet gradually. Just because we have begun riding the young horse doesn't mean that it should suddenly be given a substantial amount of grain. If you do that, you are risking colic and laminitis.

A basic rule of thumb when feeding concentrates (grain or a commercial mixed formula) is that you should never feed more than 0.75% of a horse's body weight in concentrate at any one feeding. In other words, a 1,000-pound horse should never be fed more than 7.5 pounds of concentrate at one feeding. If possible, it is better to feed a little bit of concentrate several times per day. At the least, the concentrate should be fed twice daily. Three times daily is better.

Add grain gradually.

The National Research Council has recommended that working horses be fed 0.8% to 2.0% of their body weight in forage each day and 1.0% to 2.0% of their body weight in concentrate. The higher figure for concentrate (2.0% of body weight) would be for mature horses that are working extremely hard. It would be rare that this much concentrate would be advisable for the young horse in training.

It is important to remember that the above is only a general recommendation because food needs vary horse by horse. A compact little Quarter Horse, for example, does not need as much feed as a lanky Thoroughbred or hefty warmblood.

Time and again, we have used the term observation. It is appropriate once again. If the young horse appears to be losing weight, gradually increase its feed intake. If the reverse is true, decrease the feed intake.

Prevention of overheating, appropriate cooling out procedures, and proper nutrition are highly important in the young horse maintaining a positive attitude during training.

GLOSSARY

Angular deformity — A deformity of the leg involving deviations that are seen when looking at the leg head on.

Bars of the mouth — That portion of a horse's mouth between incisors and molars where there are no teeth.

Binocular vision — The horse's ability to focus on a distant object with both eyes.

Breaking — An inappropriate term for training. Some early-day trainers did break a horse's spirit with cruel methods.

Bridle — The piece of tack that contains the bit.

Buck — The action of a horse seeking to dislodge its rider by springing into the air with the rear end being elevated.

Butt rope — Also known as rump rope. It is a rope that passes around the foal's rump so that the handler, holding both ends in his or her hand, can apply pressure to stimulate forward movement.

Cannon bone — The bone between knee and ankle in front and hock and ankle in rear.

Canter — The English term for a three-beat gait that is next in progression for speed after the trot.

Cantle — Raised rear of saddle.

Cinch — The western term for the piece of equipment that goes around the horse's barrel and holds the saddle in place.

Claustrophobia — A fear of being confined in a closed-in area.

Comfort zone index — A formula using heat and humidity readings to determine when a horse functions at its optimum capability and when it should not be exercised.

Concentrates — Grain or commercially mixed feeds.

Cue — Providing a form of stimulation to elicit a response from the horse, such as squeezing the legs to get it to move forward.

Curb bit — A bit that contains shanks that extend downward from the cheekpiece. The mouth piece may be either solid or jointed, but frequently is solid with the center being slightly raised.

D-ring — A snaffle in which the cheekpieces are formed like the letter D.

Dehydration — The point reached when the horse has lost enough body fluids whereby it can no longer cool itself nor function properly.

Desensitize — Applying the same stimulus repeatedly until the horse no longer has a negative reaction.

Direct rein — A straight pull rearward on the rein.

Dismounting — Stepping down from the saddle.

Electrolytes — The salts and minerals that are necessary for a horse's body to function properly. They are lost through sweating.

Epiphysitis — Inflammation at the growth plates of a horse's long bones.

Fight — A weapon of last resort for the horse. Only when it can't flee will it resort to using its teeth and feet to do battle.

Flexural deformity — A deformity involving the part of the leg that flexes.

Flight — A horse's first reaction to danger is to run from it.

Foal — A young horse from birth until weaning time.

Forage — Hay or grass.

Girth — The English term for the piece of equipment that goes around the horse's barrel and holds the saddle in place.

Gullet — The open area between the two sides of the pommel.

Hock — The joint of the rear leg between tibia and cannon bone.

Hypertonic sweat — Sweat of a horse that contains a significant amount of salt and potassium.

Indirect rein — A combination of a pull rearward and rein pressure on the neck.

Kicking — Lashing out with a rear foot.

Lope — The western term for a three-beat gait that is next in progression for speed after the trot.

Lunge line — A flexible, light line about 30 feet in length with a snap at one end.

Lunge whip — A whip that is 10 to 12 feet in total length, with the bottom half being rigid and the top half flexible.

Monocular vision — The horse's ability to focus on an object with one eye only.

Mounting — Stepping up onto the horse's back.

Neck rein — A form of reining used in western style riding. If the horse is being asked to turn left, the right rein will be pressed against the right side of the neck.

Nipping — A vice in which the horse uses its teeth to inflict painful bites.

Off side — The right side of the horse.

On side — The left side of the horse. (Also called near side.)

O-ring — A snaffle in which the cheekpieces are formed like the letter O.

Palpate — Using finger pressure over a horse's body. The back can be palpated to determine if the horse is suffering pain from an ill-fitting saddle.

Panels — The underside of the saddle that rests against the horse's back.

Poll — The sensitive area between a horse's ears.

Pommel — The front of the saddle.

Port — The center of the mouthpiece of a curb bit.

Rear — A movement in which a horse lifts its front end off the ground and into the air.

Reins — Equipment, usually leather, that is attached to the bit and used by the rider to direct a horse's movements in one direction or another.

Snaffle — A basic bit with two cheekpieces and a jointed mouthpiece.

Stock trailer — A trailer without individual stalls.

Striking — Lashing out with a front foot.

Throatlatch — That part of the bridle that passes around the horse's neck just behind the poll. Its purpose is to keep the bridle from being dislodged.

Trail riding — Riding a horse cross country on either marked trails or through unmarked terrain.

Training — A teaching approach that allows the horse to learn without being subjected to cruelty.

Trot — A two-beat diagonal gait: left front, right rear; right front, left rear.

Violation of space — When the horse presses into the handler's space instead of respecting it.

Walk — A four-beat gait with each foot striking the ground at a separate interval.

Weaning — Separating the foal from its dam.

Weanling — A young horse from the time it has been weaned until it reaches one year of age.

Withers — The portion of the spinal process just above the shoulders. Highly important in keeping a saddle in place.

Yearling — A young horse between one and two years of age. For breeds such as the Thoroughbred, January 1 is the universal birthday, even though a horse might be less than one year old when it reaches that date.

Yielding to pressure — Teaching the horse that it must move in response to pressure. There are many forms of pressure, ranging from a tug on the lead shank to squeezing with the legs while in the saddle.

RECOMMENDED READINGS

Ball, MA. *Understanding Basic Horse Care*. Lexington, KY: The Blood-Horse, Inc., 1999.

Dorrance, T. *True Unity, Willing Communication Between Horses and Human*. Clovis, CA: Word Dancer Press, 1994.

Ensminger, ME. (editor). *Horses and Horsemanship: Teacher's Manual*. Danville, IL: Interstate Printers and Publishers, 6th edition, 1990.

Hunt, R. et al. *Think Harmony With Horses: An In-Depth Study of Horse/Man Relationship*. Carson City, NV: America West Books, 1991.

McDonnell, S. *Understanding Horse Behavior*. Lexington, KY: The Blood-Horse, Inc., 1999.

Internet Sites for Training the Young Horse

The Horse: Your Online Guide to Equine Health Care:

http://www.thehorse.com

The American Association of Equine Practitioners' archived list
of horse articles:

http://www.aaep.org/client.htm

The HayNet, the most comprehensive equine directory on the
web:

http://www.haynet.net

Barrelhorses.com. Training tips, questions and answers:

http://www.barrelhorses.com

Quarter Horse World training tips:

http://www.quarterworld.com/demoring/index.html

A mailing list for owners of off-track Thoroughbreds. This
mailing list includes re-training tips and other advice for
ex-racehorse owners:

http://www.onelist.com/subscribe/retraintbs

The HorsesEye.com. Training tips for Paso Fino and Arabian
horses:

http://www.horseseye.com

Picture Credits

CHAPTER 1
Cheryl Manista, 10; Linda Sellnow, 13.

CHAPTER 2
Linda Sellnow, 17, 19, 20.

CHAPTER 3
Barbara D. Livingston, 26, 30; Robin Peterson, DVM, 29.

CHAPTER 4
Anne M. Eberhardt, 34; Linda Sellnow, 38.

CHAPTER 5
Anne M. Eberhardt, 41; Linda Sellnow, 43, 45.

CHAPTER 6
Linda Sellnow, 49-56, 62; Anne M. Eberhardt, 58, 60, 61.

CHAPTER 7
Linda Sellnow, 66, 67, 71.

CHAPTER 8
Linda Sellnow, 72, 74, 76-78; Anne M. Eberhardt, 79; Stephanie Church, 80.

CHAPTER 9
Shawn Hamilton, 82; Tom Hall, 87.

CHAPTER 10
Anne M. Eberhardt, 92, 93, 95.

CHAPTER 11
Dusty L. Perin, 101; Anne M. Eberhardt, 102, 103, 105.

EDITOR — JACQUELINE DUKE

ASSISTANT EDITOR — JUDY L. MARCHMAN

COVER/BOOK DESIGN — SUZANNE C. DEPP

COVER PHOTO — LINDA SELLNOW

About The Author

Les Sellnow has been a lifelong journalist and horseman. He has competed in a variety of equine disciplines, ranging from combined training to cutting and from endurance racing to western and English pleasure.

Les Sellnow

At one point, Sellnow owned and operated a training stable in Minnesota, with emphasis on preparing young horses for riding and driving careers.

As a journalist, he spent 22 years with the Brainerd (Minnesota) *Daily Dispatch*, rising from reporter to editor, winning state and national writing awards along the way. He and his wife, Linda, moved from Minnesota to Kentucky in 1984, where he served as editor of *National Show Horse* magazine and was a free-lance writer for *The Blood-Horse* magazine.

In 1994, the Sellnows moved to a ranch in the Wind River Valley near Riverton, Wyoming. Sellnow is a regular contributor to *The Horse* magazine and has had both fiction and non-fiction books published, including *Understanding Equine Lameness*, part of The Horse Health Care Library.

The Horse Health Care Library

Other Titles in The Horse Health Care Library:

- Understanding EPM
- Understanding Equine First Aid
- Understanding the Equine Foot
- Understanding Equine Lameness
- Understanding Equine Nutrition
- Understanding Laminitis
- Understanding the Foal
- Understanding the Broodmare
- Understanding Horse Behavior

- Understanding Basic Horse Care
- Understanding the Older Horse
- Understanding the Stallion
- Understanding Breeding Management
- Understanding Equine Law
- The New Equine Sports Therapy
- Horse Theft Prevention Handbook

Coming in The Horse Health Care Library:
($14.95 each)
- Understanding the Equine Eye

Videos from The Blood-Horse New Video Collection:
($39.95 each)

- Conformation: How to Buy a Winner
- First Aid for Horses
- Lameness in the Horse

- Owning Thoroughbreds
- Sales Preparation
- Insider's Guide to Buying at Auction

To order call 800-582-5604
(In Kentucky call 606-278-2361)